Discovering The Intimate Marriage

900

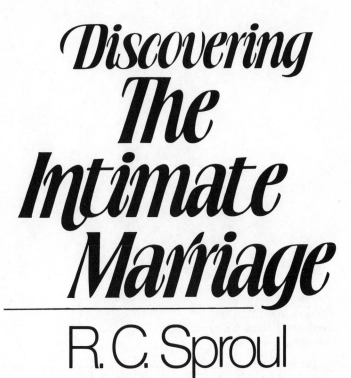

Discovering The Intimate Marriage

R. C. Sproul

*A Practical Guide
to Building a Good Marriage*

Bethany Fellowship INC.
Minneapolis, Minnesota 55438

Published by Bethany Fellowship, Inc.
6820 Auto Club Road, Minneapolis, Minnesota 55438

Printed in the United States of America

Unless otherwise indicated, Bible quotations are from the New
American Standard Bible, copyright © 1960, 1962, 1963, 1968,
1971, 1972 by The Lockman Foundation.

Library of Congress Cataloging in Publication Data:

Sproul, Robert Charles, 1939-
    Discovering the intimate marriage.

    1. Marriage.   I. Title.
HQ734.S836   301.42   75-23494
ISBN 0-87123-249-9

---

*To Sherrie and Craig,
the fruit of a happy marriage,
and once again—to Vesta*

Preface

Love and marriage—the songwriter says they go together like a horse and carriage. The aspiring goal of the romantic is love in marriage. So much hope, so much excitement, so much planning, so much feeling goes into marriage. Marriage, for many, becomes the dream of a lifetime.

So much hate, so much bitterness, so much disappointment, so much anger flows when the dream is shattered and the marriage is viewed as a failure. Does your marriage presently fulfill your former dreams? Are you not yet married but eager to be married? Are you afraid to marry because you've seen so few happy marriages?

Much, oh so much, is at stake in a marriage. Wounds come easily to the married couple, yet the joys can be enormous. The marriage dream can be beautiful or a monstrous nightmare. The hope of this author is that your marriage will be an adventure, exciting and fulfilling. This book was written not out of a need for more moralistic discussions on marriage but rather out of a conviction that marriage can be a real delight—an experience that I wouldn't trade for anything.

8

This book is designed to be a practical guide for marriage. It is purposefully nontechnical. It will not serve as a detailed manual for problem-solving. It is but a general introduction to basic patterns of married life. Questions are given at the end of each chapter to stimulate discussion between those already married and those contemplating marriage. I am hopeful that the book will be helpful for laymen involved in small group studies.

An attempt is made in this book to apply basic biblical principles to marriage. If these principles are utterly foreign to you, I hope you will examine them carefully and practically that the wisdom of God may be discovered.

Thanks are in order to Dr. William White for the careful reading of the manuscript and the many helpful suggestions he has given. Thanks also to Pat Zornan and Mary Semach for their help in the preparation of the manuscript.

Contents

1
Communication in Marriage

Undoubtedly the problem of communication in marriage started a long time ago. It would not surprise me to learn that the first man to say, "My wife doesn't understand me," was Adam. It all started in the primordial garden when Adam asked Eve if she ate of the forbidden tree and Eve replied, "Tree? What tree?" The problem was compounded when God discovered their transgression and called Adam aside to interrogate him. For three hours Eve waited in solitude for the decision of her Creator. Anxiety increased by the minute until at last Adam emerged from the summit meeting that would decide human destiny. Breathlessly Eve rushed to her husband and gasped, "What did He say?" Adam shrugged his shoulders and said, "Oh, nothing!" Things have been going downhill ever since.

The subject of communication in marriage is a difficult one, perhaps impossible. Someone has said that to discover the secret of communication, one must undertake the Herculean task of sailing between Scylla and Chrybidis, using the sword of

Damacles to cut the Gordian knot that it may fit its Procustean Bed! (Whoever said that ought to be shot.) Communication is not always easy. It involves work, pain, sensitivity, patience and great care. Communicating is often a burdensome task, but a task that must be accomplished for a marriage to be complete. When communication falters, the marriage is in trouble. When it fails altogether, the marriage is virtually doomed.

Communication is, above all, a means of knowing. In marriage it means, simply, the knowing of two people. The goal of communication is knowledge—not abstract, theoretical, impersonal knowledge but personal knowledge, the knowledge of intimacy. In biblical categories the essence of marriage is expressed in the intimacy of knowing and loving.

When the Old Testament writers describe the sex act, the usual term used is a form of the verb "to know." We read that Adam "knew" his wife and she conceived. Abraham knew his wife, etc. What is the writer trying to convey? The Bible is not trying to suggest that reproduction takes place by the ability to recognize or distinguish one person from another. When Adam "knew" his wife it means more than that they had been formally introduced. Nor is the biblical writer given to euphemism when he uses the term "knew." It would be out of character for an Old Testament writer to avoid candor in favor of euphemism. No, when the Old Testament speaks of sexual union in terms of knowing, it is because *knowing* in every sense of the word is at the heart of marriage. To be known and still be loved is one of the supreme goals of marriage.

Many of us think that if people really knew us they would not like us. Others think, however, if people knew us well enough to understand us, perhaps they would like us. Most of us probably feel a little of both. We would like to be really known—but there remains the nagging fear that if we are known, we won't be loved. Before the Fall, Adam and Eve enjoyed their life in Eden, "naked and unashamed." After the Fall they became aware of their nakedness and hid themselves in shame. In their guilt they didn't want God to see them, becoming fugitives from His gaze. Yet in an act of astonishing grace, God provided clothes for His embarrassed creatures and covered their nakedness. But the desire for the original state of being naked and unashamed remained with Adam and Eve. They wanted their nakedness and their shame hidden, yet yearned for a safe place to be naked. They yearned for a place where they could take off their clothes and be known without fear. God provided that place in the institution of marriage. God gave them a place where they could have "intercourse," which, of course, is a synonym for verbal communication.

Communication involves a kind of nakedness. In some situations, nakedness can be very embarrassing. At other times, it can be supremely exhilarating. So it is with communication. When communication is carried on in a proper way in marriage, it yields unspeakable pleasure. When it fails, the result is two people going back into hiding.

The biblical example of proper communication in marriage is seen in the way God relates to His people. It is not by accident that the primary image in the Bible of the relationship between God and His people is the image of marriage. In the Old Testament Israel is the bride of Yahweh; in the New Testament the Church is the bride of Christ. When God reveals himself and communicates His love to His bride, the bride rejoices. When the bride spurns God's revelation and seeks other gods, she perishes in her spiritual adultery.

To be known of God is the highest goal of human existence. To know that God knows everything about me and yet loves me is indeed my ultimate consolation. What a comfort to know I cannot "pull the wool" over God's eyes—there's no point in ever trying. The human institution of marriage should mirror that consolation. The more we are able to reveal ourselves to our life partners and still be loved, the more we are able to understand what a relationship to God is all about. The greatest consolation I have in this world is the knowledge that my wife knows me better than any person on this planet, and—guess what? She loves me.

Knowledge and Intimacy

In the sixties our nation experienced what has become known as "the sex revolution." The free-speech movement at Berkeley triggered a mass student reaction against traditional values and customs regarding sex. Crusades for "free love," "sex without marriage," etc., steamrolled across the land. A common protest was that the older generation was a generation of hypocrites. To them sex was a hush-hush thing, not openly exposed to public scrutiny. The symbol of the older generation was the lock on the bedroom door. When the adolescent

of the sixties discovered that babies don't come
from storks, he looked at the lock on the door and
the drawn shades and cried, "Hypocrisy!" What
our children call hypocrisy, we call intimacy.
Hopefully our children will learn to understand
the difference.

In modern usage the term "intimacy" suggests
merely a sexual relationship. But the word goes
deeper than that. In its broader meaning intimacy
indicates a familiar relationship that moves beyond the external and the superficial and pene-
trates the innermost dimensions of our life. Marriage was designed to be a relationship of intimacy.
Total intimacy embraces far more than the sexual
aspect. In fact, there must be a kind of intimacy
preceding sexual union if that union is going to
be of lasting value. Intercourse with a prostitute
is intercourse without intimacy. One can have sex
without intimacy. But one cannot have communication in the biblical sense of "knowing" without
intimacy.

Communication and Listening

One essential ingredient of communication is
listening. Without listening there is no communication. Communication simply cannot take place
on a one-way street. Not only must we learn to
listen, but we must learn to listen carefully. There
is the old illustration of the three sermons that
are preached each Sunday. First is the sermon
the people hear; second is the sermon the preacher
thought he gave; and third is the actual sermon
given. This discrepancy between what is said and
what people hear was brought home to me recently

in a lecture situation. After I finished my lecture I opened the meeting for discussion. Someone immediately asked about a certain word in my lecture. I said I couldn't remember using that word at all. Someone else chimed in and said, with certainty, that I had used another word. Immediately the class was divided on the issue. About half of the people said I used one word and the other half argued that I used the other. I meekly suggested that I didn't use either of the words in dispute. But by this time, of course, I imagined that I must have used one of the two words in question. Finally, to resolve the debate, I played back the recording of that portion of the lecture. To everyone's consternation, including my own, I had used neither of the two words in dispute. We all had a lesson in listening.

In marriage, real communication often demands listening beyond or "between the lines" of words being spoken. For various reasons we frequently are given to indirect discourse. Instead of saying what we mean and meaning what we say, we attempt to communicate via hints and innuendos. Then we wonder why nobody understands us.

Not too long ago my wife (hereafter to be mentioned by her name, Vesta—I intend to refer to her frequently for purposes of illustration) left the house to visit a friend. I said, "Why are you going to Kathy's?" She replied that she was going to get a home permanent. I asked her for the hundredth time since we'd been married, "Why don't you go to the hairdresser like everyone else?" She carefully explained that she didn't need to go to a professional hairdresser because Kathy did a perfectly good job, and she did it free of charge. I couldn't argue with that so I dropped the matter. But I was upset. Vesta couldn't figure out why. Finally, I broke down and told her the real reason I "hinted" at being displeased with the home-permanent routine. I said, "I can't tell the difference between a professional permanent and a home permanent. That's not the point. My pride is involved in this. I can afford to pay the hairdresser bill. You make me feel inadequate as a provider." As soon as I expressed my feelings directly instead of by hints, I saw how foolish they were. But Vesta didn't treat them as foolish, asking, "Why didn't you ever tell me that?" The point is, of course, I had been telling her that for years, but I was saying it so obliquely she couldn't possibly "hear" it. Reading between the lines is one thing; reading your spouse's mind is quite another.

I am not seeking to establish an axiom that all wives must always go to a professional hairdresser for their permanents or their husbands will feel insecure. Rather the point is twofold: First, we must be careful to avoid discourse that is so vague and indirect that no one could get the point; and, secondly, it may be helpful to ask yourself the question, "Why does my spouse often bring up this issue? What is really being said?"

Communication and Gift-Giving

One vital checkpoint to test the level of communication in marriage is the matter of gift exchange. Hints fly at will as we seek subtle ways of letting our partners know what we want for Christmas or birthdays. Vesta is the practical type.

Christmas would come, and she would present me with a beautifully wrapped package that would bring back the exciting memories of boyhood. I would open the package and find three white shirts. I would say, "Oh boy! White shirts. Just what I need, Honey!" (While I was thinking, "White shirts! I can buy them anytime. I don't want white shirts. I want golf clubs.") Being careful to disguise my feelings, I would go on about how great the white shirts were. I was such a good actor that the next year I would get *five* white shirts. For years she gave me what I needed, not what I wanted.

I tried hinting to Vesta by giving her extravagant gifts. Throwing caution to the wind, I would run out and buy her an expensive new coat, straining our bank account to the limit. I'd have the coat expertly gift-wrapped and present it to her with gusto. She would open the gift and exclaim, "Honey, it's beautiful, but we can't afford this. I need a vacuum sweeper." What happened in this situation is that both of us assumed the other person wanted the kind of gift we wanted. We were projecting our own desires on our partner. When we finally discussed this matter honestly, I got my golf clubs and she got her sweeper.

The Hide-Go-Seek Game

A serious barrier to communication is deception. That lying destroys credibility and violates trust is obvious. But more subtle means of obscuring the truth may also be destructive to effective communication. When we begin to play hide-and-seek in the most important context God provides for openness, we are in trouble. The game of deception is established on the mythological premise that "what she [he] doesn't know, won't hurt her [him]."

Let the following illustration suffice: I came home from the golf course one afternoon. Vesta asked me if I had a good time. I recounted the events of the day with delight. Then she asked the provocative question, "How much money did you spend?" I gave her a proper accounting of green-fees, caddy-fees, a couple of new golf balls (that contributed finally to T. S. Elliot's "Barren Wasteland"), and then added $5 for a lesson from the pro. Vesta exclaimed, "We can't afford $5 for golf lessons!" I meekly surrendered to her feelings and changed the subject. In the weeks that followed, my golf game improved a bit; and I kept thinking, "Two or three more lessons, and I would really have this game together." (Hope springs eternal in the golfer's breast. . . .) So I went to the pro and had three more lessons. Only this time I didn't tell Vesta about it and carefully instructed the pro not to send any bills to my house but to settle the bill with me privately. He smiled in agreement, saying he had to do that for a lot of the guys. Unfortunately, the pro forgot to relay the message to his secretary. Arriving home one day, Vesta met me at the door with a knowing look on her face and the bill in her hand. I was dumbfounded, and then all I could do was stand there and laugh. Sternly she said, "It's not funny." I replied, "I know, that's why I'm laughing!" (I didn't know what else to do.) She asked, "Why did you deceive me?" I gave her the myth of "I figured what you didn't know wouldn't hurt you." She said, "Well, it does hurt me, and it hurts me even more that you felt you had to hide it from me." I told her that I didn't particularly enjoy feeling that I had to hide it from her either. But she was violated by my subterfuge. This experience was painful for both of us because I chose deception over truth.

Communicating Love

Perhaps the question most frequently asked by the wife is, "Do you love me?" Standard replies are often less than helpful. Answers like "Of course" or "I married you, didn't I?" or even worse, "Wait until tonight, and I'll show you," do very little to communicate love. Communicating a desire for sexual gratification is not the same thing as communicating love. Women are very well aware that a man doesn't have to be in love to be able to enjoy sex. One sage maintained that a woman needs to be told she is loved in 365 different ways every year. The truth of this hyperbole, however, is that women usually notice seemingly small expressions of affection. (And so do men.) Husbands must discover what makes their wives feel loved and vice versa.

In my house the issue of communicating love usually resolves down to apparently insignificant or even "irrational" things. We have a perennial crisis over the lipstick issue. It seems as if all of my insecurities about my wife's affection for me are wrapped up in a small tube of lipstick. I know (without hyperbole) that I've asked my wife 10,000 times to put on lipstick. Whenever I see her without lipstick, I take it as a personal insult. (That's 10,000 personal insults, which is a lot of insults.) When the insults become so frustrating that I can't stand it any longer, I give vent to my exasperation by saying, "When are you going to start wearing lipstick?" The normal reply, "When *you* start picking up your clothes!"

Then there is the washcloth issue. Some wives are neat; others are fussy; but mine is punctilious. It seems to me that she has a neurotic concern for neatness in detail. She thinks I have an uncontrollable passion for making messy what she has made neat. I say, "How can I tell you I love you?" She says, "By not rolling up the washcloth in a ball when you're done with it and throwing it in the sink." How unromantic. It would be so much more exciting to demonstrate my affection by slaying a few dragons or even making a birdie for her on the golf course. Who wants to show love by hanging up washcloths? Yet when I take the extra few seconds required to wring out the washcloth and hang it neatly on the towel rack, my wife has been told that she is loved—and told in a way that communicates. I've let her know that I care about her labor and that I don't regard her task of housekeeping as insignificant.

Learning to Know

Learning isn't always a difficult enterprise. There are patented shortcuts to all kinds of fields of inquiry. A general acquaintance of many areas can be gleaned via casual involvement, exposure or by a kind of intellectual osmosis. However, if one wants to move beyond a level of general acquaintance to the level of genuine expertise, the shortcut methods will not avail. To be an expert in any field of knowledge requires intensive study.

Time and effort are necessary for the acquisition of in-depth knowledge.

Unfortunately many people approach the task of learning to know their spouses in a very cavalier spirit. No serious effort to study their partners is ever made. However, marriage brings to a person a unique opportunity and sober responsibility to be an expert in the knowledge of his spouse. To be an expert in the knowledge of your mate requires concentrated and conscious study. For a man to understand more about the law of thermodynamics than he understands about his wife is to be guilty of gross neglect of duty. Of course, I am not recommending the reduction of your partner to the level of a specimen to be analyzed under a microscope, nor the cold, calculated analysis of a disinterested spectator. To be always seeking the hidden meaning behind every word of gesture would be absurd. But I'm not really worried about the eventuality of such an extreme. That's not the problem that is systematically disintegrating the American home. Our problem is not that people are working too hard to know their mates; our problem is that too many people are barely trying at all.

The television series the Newlywed Game and other such shows that match husbands' and wives' answers, etc., seem funny, but really they are tragic. They reveal not the rare or unusual but the commonplace. They provide an ominous warning that couples simply do not know each other. Somebody is not doing his homework.

To make a conscious effort to gain insight into a human being is not simply a sober responsibility in marriage, but a very special privilege. Few areas of study can be so exciting and so fruitful. If it is a labor of love, that love will only be intensified.

The death of my father during my teenage years was an event of momentous trauma in my life. Though many of the memories of the events surrounding his death are now dimmed and obscured, and most of the content of the eulogy by our family minister is vague in my mind, one thing stands out sharply. The minister made mention of the distinctive character of my father's footsteps. He said that if he saw my father walking at a distance, he immediately recognized him by his footfall. He said that if he heard my father approaching his study, he knew who it was by the sound of his footsteps. In a word, he knew my father by his walk. The thing that surprised me about all this was that my father had no immediately observable unusual gait. He had no limp or unusual heaviness of walking. I had never noticed a thing strange or unusual about the way he walked. Yet after the service my mother expressed her amazement that the pastor shared her knowledge of this less than obvious characteristic of my father. The minister had over two thousand members in his congregation; he knew everyone of those members by name. He made a diligent effort to know his people. If that minister had manifested nothing else of the nature of Christ, he at least manifested the extraordinary virtue of the Good Shepherd who knows His sheep.

If a minister can learn to know two thousand people, why is it so difficult for us to learn to know one person? When the Apostle Paul exhorts the women of Ephesus to be in submission to their husbands, he uses the term "own." Be subject to your *own* husbands. The word is *idios* from which comes "idiosyncracies" or even the word "idiot." (I sometimes play a bit with the text by encouraging women to submit to their "idiot" husbands!) Actually, we know the difference between idiots and idiosyncracies. The idiosyncrasies of our partners are worth knowing, for in them we can discover the uniqueness of the one who is our "own."

There are countless easy and nonthreatening ways that a husband and wife can get to know each other. My wife and I invent little games to learn more about each other. While driving or sitting around the house, etc., I'll ask questions like, "If I could be anything in the world besides what I am, what would I be?" Simple little questions like these often stimulate lengthy in-depth discussions that are very helpful. The answers are often quite interesting and illuminating.

The task never ends as new insights reveal more of the complexities that make a human being what he or she is. My wife and I have been together for 22 years, and yet a few days ago she made a surprising discovery. About five minutes before I was scheduled to lecture to a rather sizable group of people, my wife handed me a letter from an old friend. To my shock, the letter contained a very angry tirade directed at me. The personal attack was very painful to me but after reading the letter I gave no indication of its effect. I calmly handed the letter to Vesta and matter-of-factly commented, "He is very angry." I went at once to the podium and delivered the lecture. After the meeting I told her how relieved I was that the lecture was over as I had barely made it through.

My stomach was churning, and as hard as I tried I could not push the letter out of mind. During the lecture I felt like a zombie—an aura of unreality surrounded me. It was as if I were merely a spectator rather than the speaker. Vesta's response to the episode was amazement. She said, "I had no idea anything was bothering you. I never detected the slightest hint that anything was wrong." Had I not revealed to my wife the real pain of the situation, we would have lived through a small part of our lives together completely out of touch with each other.

How deeply aware are you of your partner's clothes? It is nonsense to affirm that "clothes make the man," but it is equally foolish to assume that clothes have no effect on personality, attitudes, and moods. When a woman wears a new dress, she often not only looks nice but she may feel better as well. Military requirements of "spit and polish" are not designed for appearance only but to help instill a snappy spirit of alertness and coordinated discipline. Uniforms function not only as a symbol of a particular occupation, but they help to create an atmosphere conducive to the functioning of the persons within that occupation. Witness the outfits and listen to the comments of the local golfers: "If I can't play like a golfer at least I can look like one." One of the all-time great golfers of yesteryear is Gene Sarazen. Sarazen is now in his seventies and still plays golf. However, he will not play golf unless he is wearing knickers, a white shirt and a tie. People smile at his old-time outfit until they see him hit the ball. Sarazen says he feels as if he can't play well in a modern outfit.

The feelings that are associated with clothes

came home to me rudely when I went out for football in high school. Our school was a major football power. That year the team won the Western Pennsylvania Championship. Consequently, the competition was keen for every position. Those of us who were sophomores had no expectations of making the varsity team, but we did have dreams of making the squad and consolidating our positions for future glory. The coach told me I had a pretty good lock on the starting job of J.V. quarterback and even a good shot at back-up quarterback to our star senior quarterback. I checked into summer camp with confidence and optimism. But then the moment of truth came. We lined up in the locker room to receive our practice equipment and uniforms. The seniors went first, followed by the juniors, and finally the sophomores. To further complicate matters, we lined up alphabetically. If only my name had started with "A." By the time I got to the equipment manager he was at the bottom of his stock. I was issued an oversized pair of lineman's shoulder pads, a helmet two sizes larger than my head and pants a full three sizes too large. I had to use my belt from my street clothes to keep my pants up. What a spectacle! When I was fully dressed I looked like something from Notre Dame (the Hunchback!). I looked less like Johnny Unitas than Alice Blue Gown. What made it worse was I felt like Alice Blue Gown. How can a quarterback give an impression of smooth ball-handling in an outfit like that? I felt miserable—and played that way.

Not only can ill-fitting clothes or uniforms make us feel and act miserable, but the converse is true as well. If your wife doesn't "feel like a woman," maybe a check of the wardrobe is in order. Of course, clothes per se will not save a marriage or cause one to disintegrate. But it is a very serious matter when a wife does not feel like a woman, and clothes can certainly contribute to that feeling.

Many men have no idea what their wives' dress size is. When a husband takes no interest in his wife's clothes, the wife inevitably feels less than a woman. Shopping together can be an exciting enterprise as new vistas of beauty are explored. Care must be taken against talking a woman into wearing what might violate her canons of modesty and taste. But the point is this. Clothing can be a vital point of marital communication. An aside to Christians: God calls us to modesty of dress. But there is a difference between being modest and being dull and drab. The light of the world should be attractive and the salt of the world tasty.

How Well Do You Communicate?

I've devised a very simple test that I use with couples to give them some visible barometer of their communication quotient. I ask the people to list ten things on a sheet of paper that they would like to have their partners do for them, ten needs or desires that can be fulfilled by the spouse. It isn't necessary that these be needs that are presently not fulfilled. The idea is to list things that are important to the mate. The other restriction is that the items be listed in concrete terms. No abstractions like "make me feel loved" are allowed. After this list is finished I ask the people to use the other side of the paper for another list. The second list is an enumeration of the things you think your mate would like you to do for him. When both lists are completed I ask the couples to exchange papers and compare them. If all twenty items on each paper match, then I recommend that the couple open a clinic and go into the marriage counseling business. (But I've never seen that, or anything near it, take place.) If none of the items match, the implications are obvious. This indicates a very serious communication problem that demands immediate attention and counseling. What most couples will learn from such a simple test is that there is room for improvement in communication and the test itself may be a catalyst for that to take place. Further implications of this little test will be explored later in this book.

The Path Test

The path test is also a game-playing test that is sometimes used as a party game. It, however, can be threatening and is capable of being misleading. It is not scientifically impeccable and so must be used with a high degree of caution. It is a game of imagination where one's fantasies are allowed to run free. The person is asked to imagine himself walking alone along a path. (No further details are supplied except by the imagination.) Then the person is to write down his immediate mental images to the following points of the narrative. "You see a key on the path. What does it look like? and what would you do with it?" The people then put into writing their description and reaction to the key. Next the person is asked to describe a vase that he finds on the path and note his reactions to it. As the trip proceeds, the person then is told he meets a bear on the path. Again a description of the bear and the person's reaction are noted. Going on down the path the person then comes to some water. Again the water is described by the participant as well as a narrative of what is done with the water. At this point, the trip may either be terminated or other incidents of little importance tacked on. What follows is an analysis of the symbolism involved.

Supposedly the key is the universal symbol of education. The person's description of the key reflects his inner feelings about education. The scientifically or technically oriented person will tend to picture a very functional key such as a house key. The romantic will picture a very ornate, perhaps mysterious key. The pragmatist or materialist will tend toward a car key. Though the symbols are not absolutely accurate, they can be provocative aids to in-depth discussion about education.

Moving to the vase is a move to more dangerous ground. The vase is supposed to symbolize one's life partner. On more than one occasion I have witnessed people expressing violent hostility toward their imaginary vase, saying they imagine smashing it to pieces. Some wax very romantic about the beauty and the texture of the vase. (My wife saw a big strong vase that was cracked!!)

The vision of the bear is supposed to symbolize the way one deals with obstacles and problems. Some people run, others hide; some walk circumspectly by the bear, while others stand absolutely still. Some people imagine roaring grizzlies standing on their hind legs, while others see cute little cubs that represent no threat whatsoever. (I saw a vicious black bear which I engaged in hand-to-hand combat.)

The symbol of water is the most provocative of all. The theory is that water is the universal symbol of sex. Not only what kind of water people see, but what they do with it is significant. One couple who came to me for marriage counseling both indicated that they "saw" ugly, stagnant pools of water which they carefully avoided. Conversely, when giving this test to a self-confessed nymphomaniac, she saw an ocean (in the middle of the woods!) with violent rolling waves. She said she dove in the water and it violently tossed her around and hurt her, but she still found it exhilarating. Many people, particularly females, visualize a beautiful mountain stream. They enjoy dipping their toes in the water but say the water is too cold to go swimming.

Again, let me remind the reader that the path test can be a very enjoyable way of exploring inner feelings, but can also be both inaccurate and threatening.

Communication in Sex

As I indicated earlier, this dimension of communication is vital to a successful marriage relationship. Intercourse in the full sense of the word is involved here. The dynamics of sex are so crucial to communication in marriage that I will devote a separate chapter to the subject. In a nation that seems to be preoccupied with sex and in an age that boasts of free and open discussion of the subject, it is a total anomaly that widespread ignorance still exists. But it does, and the results are frequently devastating. In this area as in the others, a conscious effort of study is necessary for effective communication.

A close friend and fellow-laborer related the following incident. He had been away from his wife for six weeks while on a speaking tour, etc. Needless to say, he missed his wife keenly. Upon his arrival home from the airport he didn't even bother to unpack his suitcase. Leaving it by the front door, he eagerly embraced his wife and took her straight to the bedroom. After a half hour of passionate love his wife said to him, "Honey?" He replied, "Yes, dear, what is it?" "Honey, did you remember to shut the garage door?" The incredulous husband said, "How long have you been thinking about the garage door?" She answered innocently, "Oh, about twenty-five minutes!" Needless to say, the passionate love was squelched.

Conscious study of your marriage partner involves the physiological dimension as well as emotional and psychological. One of the frequent techniques employed by sex rehabilitation and counseling clinics is the technique of physiological exploration. For example a couple may be instructed to be alone for forty-eight hours and spend this time in verbal conversation and physical exploration of each other's body. The condition attached to the assignment is that there may not be any sexual intercourse. (Many persons with serious sexual communication problems are relieved to hear that actual intercourse is not a part of their preliminary therapy.) Most couples find that the most difficult aspect of the assignment

32

is keeping the no-intercourse rule. When the preliminary details of communication are followed
it is difficult to resist their natural culmination.
That, of course, is the point of the therapy. To
know one's spouse fully is know him or her in
body, mind, and soul.

The Rape of the Soul

To seek to know your partner is vital to communication. But the quest for that knowledge cannot be carried out with ruthless coercion. Though
we must encourage each other toward mutual self-
revelation, we must guard scrupulously against
manipulation. Self-exposure is not always easy,
and the insensitive prober can do violence to the
soul.

Recently I said to Vesta, "I want to know your
soul, totally and completely." She reacted de-
fensively, "Oh, no! I want some privacy. I want
some part of me that is all mine." That provoked
quite a discussion. I was somewhat bewildered.
Thoughts like, "Why doesn't she trust me?" and
"What is she hiding, and why is she hiding it?"
went racing through my head. As we talked it
out, certain things became clear. She expressed
her desire to be a genuine helpmate to me. She
then explained her feeling about the crisis that
role can produce—the crisis of the loss of personal
identity. She said she didn't want to be merely
"Mrs." Sproul; she wanted an identity of her own.
She wisely reminded me that the biblical union
of two people into "one flesh" did not involve the
annihilation of personal identity. The unity of marriage is not to be monistic but a unity in duality.

I expressed the desire to know her soul in order to love it, but she had gotten the impression that I wanted that knowledge in order to possess her soul and exploit it. That's the fear, and the danger is real. She will reveal her soul only when she is sure it is safe. If I want that knowledge, I must labor to establish that safety. Any other approach would be rape.

Questions for Discussion

1. How well do I know my partner?
2. Do I want to know and be known more intimately?
3. Am I a good listener? Do I feel that my partner is a good listener?
4. What kind of gifts do I give? What kind of gifts do I like to receive?
5. What kind of things do I hide from my spouse?
6. How do I show my love? How would my partner like me to show my love?
7. Am I a disciplined student of the knowledge of my spouse?
8. Do I like my partner's clothes?
9. How did we do on the communication test?
10. What did the path test reveal to me?

2
Problems in Marriage

Even the best marriages are beset with problems. Often the difference between a healthy marriage and a defective one is not the number or severity of problems encountered but in the way problems are dealt with. Thus, the first problem we must examine is the problem of solving problems.

The Problem of Problem-Solving

Dr. Jay Adams, author of the widely read book *Competent to Counsel*, once related the following anecdote in my presence. A man was driving along a highway in his expensive new car. Suddenly he noted that the red warning light marked "oil" on his instrument panel was flashing. Ignoring the warning issued in the car owner's manual, stating that in the event of the flashing red light the driver should stop his car immediately, he continued merrily along. After a while the constant flashing of the light began to annoy him and irritated his senses, though he tried to think of something else. He even turned the instrument panel lights off, but to no avail—the light kept blinking. Finally the solution came to him. He reached into the glove compartment and, pulling out a hammer, proceeded to smash the light to pieces. Peaceful at last, the driver continued on in his euphoric oblivion until his car burned up.

Adam's analogy is obvious. He describes the method all too often employed in marital problem-solving. The issues of the marriage are ignored or avoided until they mount to explosive proportions. Problems that are ignored are not solved. There are many ways to ignore problems. One way is to deny that they exist. We can retreat into a philosophy of illusion that denies the reality of evil. Many such philosophies have been formulated in world history—some have even been given a religious coating. The reasoning goes something like this: All evil is illusory. Problems are evil. Therefore problems don't exist. There is no sense worrying about what doesn't exist.

I once gave a lecture to a group of college students on the problem of evil. During the discussion that followed I was challenged by a young man who believed that evil didn't exist. He was distressed because he felt I was misleading the people by not telling the truth about evil. I asked the student, "Do you think it is a good thing that I am standing here telling these people that evil really exists?" He replied at once, "No, I don't!" Then I put forward the question that was obvious to everyone in the room except the young man: "Do you think that what I am telling these people is bad?" Finally the young man got the point and slouched back in his chair somewhat embarrassed.

Other couples may recognize that evil exists and that problems are real in general but insist that they just don't have any. Here the problem with problems is the problem of pride. To admit to yourself that you have a problem is often to admit to a particular failure. Often in marriage counseling we are forced to deal with only one member of the marriage partnership because the other one is too stubborn to admit the need for help. Not always, but often it is the husband who is the stubborn one. The male who works out his existence in a competitive world deals with success and failure every day. Perhaps because of this factor he doesn't want to deal with the threat of failure at home. He considers it beneath his dignity to go to a counselor for help. He says, "I don't have any problems." This type of man will sometimes "allow" the wife to go to the counselor. His pride is so great that he has deluded himself into thinking all the problems stem from her. In this case when the car burns up, the driver blames the mechanic or the manufactuer and argues that he did the best he could with his little hammer.

Another way to sidestep problems and acquire an aura of spiritual strength at the same time is to "praise the Lord" for them. This can be a very subtle cop-out. To be sure, the Christian is called to recognize the sovereignty of God over all his life and be aware that God promises to work sanctification and redemption out of all tribulation. There is a genuine sense in which Christians are to be grateful to God in the midst of trial. But this can be distorted into a flippant gimmick that is used as an escape hatch from dealing responsibly with problems. Maybe a better way is to "praise the Lord" and get busy solving the problem.

So we see that problems can be ignored by denying their reality or by minimizing their importance, reducing them to a less serious dimension than they really are. Conversely, problems can be overstated and exaggerated beyond all reality. Hysteria is not an effective method of dealing with problems. Overstatement or exaggeration of problems is really only another subtle method of refusing to face the problem as it is.

If problems are to be solved, they must first be identified with some degree of accuracy. This requires a sober, honest evaluation of the situation. If you are incapable of such an analysis, then it is imperative that you cooperate with a counselor who is competent to do it for you.

Once the problem is identified it must then be solved. It is not difficult to solve problems, but it may be difficult to solve them properly. Not all solutions are good ones. Our car owner solved his problem of the blinking light quite readily, but his solution caused problems that were worse than the first. As we solve our problems of the present we cannot determine with certainty the effects of the solution in the future. But we must consider the possible and probable long-range effects of the solution. Again, Dr. Adams offers an anecdote that illustrates the importance of long-range planning.

In a lecture in California Dr. Adams considered the biblical narrative of Abraham and Lot. It seems that the two men were involved in a large scale cattle-ranching enterprise. But the Scripture succinctly tells the story: "And the land was not able to bear them, that they might dwell together"

(Gen. 13:6). A feud developed between Abraham's cowboys and Lot's cowboys, and the place wasn't big enough for both. Abraham wanted to salvage his relationship with Lot so he proposed a solution. He suggested that they separate their men and herds, and he gave Lot his choice of the east or the west. Lot looked west and all he saw was rugged terrain that would make grazing difficult and driving to market an enormous problem. He looked to the east and saw the well-watered plain of Jordan, right next to the city. There he could fatten his herds with ease and have no trouble getting the produce to market. For Lot, the choice was easy. He went east to the city and left Abraham to eke out an existence in the west. Wise choice? Lot forgot to consider a few items like: "Where will my family go to church? What kind of environment will be there for my children?" Lot moved his family to Sodom. Sodom was a great place to raise cattle. . . . Later when his daughters were violated, the city destroyed, and his wife turned to a pillar of salt, Lot went to his friendly minister and asked, "Where did I go wrong?" By the way, Abraham's family did all right.

Christ told His disciples not to be anxious about tomorrow, but He never said not to *consider* tomorrow. Intelligent problem-solving demands careful consideration of the future effects of present solutions. All too frequently I am called upon to minister to Christian parents who are confused and hurt because their children have repudiated their faith while being away at college. They can't seem to figure out what happened to provoke such a change in their children. Then I ask them where the students are going to school. The schools named are often colleges and universities that are notorious for their militant stance against the Christian faith. I then ask why the parents sent their youngsters to that particular college or university. The answers I hear are terrifying. "It has such a beautiful campus." "It is so close to home." "They have a sorority or fraternity like I was in." "I went there myself and it was a wonderful Christian college twenty-five years ago." Incredible, but true. Where a young person goes to college will have far-reaching effects on the shaping of his thinking, values, etc. Can the color of the grass on campus possibly be an intelligent basis for selecting a college? Consider the effects.

One of the most important steps in solving a marriage problem is talking about it (choosing wisely the time and place) with each other. As we've already noted, many problems have their origin in, and are accentuated by, failure in communication. When the problems are discussed the couple must learn to talk *to* each other rather than past each other. Accusations and lengthy speeches of defense are indicators that people are talking past each other rather than to each other. If you cannot come to an agreement about how to solve a problem, it may be helpful to submit to arbitration and mediation. A third party without a vested interest in the dispute may be an important catalyst to get you to talk *to* each other.

Often in counseling situations I talk with couples separately before seeing them together. After hearing two people describe their situation separately, I wonder if they know each other at all. When bringing the couples together for counseling I try to get them to learn the use of one little word. The key word for understanding each other is the word "why?" This word, if used properly, can unlock a safe full of knowledge. If used improperly, it can be a battle-cry. It is one thing to ask calmly, "Why did you say that?" or "Why do you feel like that?" It is another thing to use the word as a belligerent challenge, shouting, "Why!!?"

To solve problems, they must be identified, faced, discussed, a solution agreed upon that takes into account the future, and finally the solution acted upon. This method isn't foolproof, but it promises a high rate of success.

My Problem Is Unique and Insoluble

So often people are paralyzed by their problem and give up in despair before they tackle it because they think they are the only ones in the world to ever encounter that particular situation. When Neil Armstrong stepped backwards down a ladder in outer space onto the moon, he had a problem that was somewhat unique. No one before ever encountered that particular problem, but his task was not utterly unique. Maybe no one had ever descended a ladder onto the moon before, but millions of people have descended ladders. Not only are your problems not utterly unique, but they are problems that are being dealt with successfully every day. Maybe you've never met anybody with your particular problem, but chances are you haven't met everybody yet. In thinking your problem is utterly unique, you may have another problem you haven't considered—arrogance.

I frequently encounter this attitude in theological students. They've wrestled with a thorny theological problem for a while and have not come up with a solution. Consequently, they come to the conclusion that the problem is insoluble. Granted, there are many perplexing questions of theology that remain unanswered. But they are far less than many students think. The arrogance lies at this point: "Because I can't answer this question, that must mean the question can't be answered or hasn't been answered by anyone else." One of the purposes of education is to study with professors who have spent a great deal of time examining their fields of inquiry and who, hopefully, can answer a few more questions than the students can. I don't know how many times I've discovered answers by simply consulting people more knowledgeable than myself. If you have a problem that you can't solve by yourself, at least give yourself the benefit of consulting experts before you conclude that the question cannot be answered or the problem solved.

The Problem of Anger

How we deal with anger will have a significant effect on our ability to solve marital problems. Most fights in the marriage estate are not produced by a simple, bare hostility. Anger is a very complex dimension of human experience and is closely related to frustration, disappointment, and other similar aspects. Dealing with anger can be greatly facilitated by seeking to understand what it is and what it involves. You might begin by asking yourself the simple question, "What makes me angry?" Take a pencil and a piece of paper and list your pet peeves or the things that make you really angry. Then probe further asking yourself, "Why does this make me so angry?" How do you handle frustration? Why? How do you handle disappointment? Why? The answers to these basic questions will help you move a long way toward dealing effectively with your anger.

There is often a close, even progressive, relationship between frustration, disappointement, and anger. Notice the obvious feeling degrees of a small child who tries to hammer a peg into a difficult hole. You watch the frustration mount until it gives way to anger and he throws the hammer or kicks the playschool stand. Notice the frequent eruptions of tempers in the closing minutes of a football game when the losing team allows their frustrations and disappointment to give way to anger. When your husband comes home from a frustrating day at work, you will probably find him on the rim of anger and somewhat "touchy." If your wife snaps at you when you walk in the door, it's a pretty safe bet that she has had a super-frustrating day with the kids. Anger doesn't take place in a vacuum. There is much about anger that needs to be understood.

The first thing that needs to be understood about anger is that it isn't always a bad thing. Many people, especially Christians, have the mistaken notion that anger is intrinsically evil. Consequently, much guilt is experienced with respect to anger. The idea that a Christian is never allowed to be angry is a demonic myth that has a tendency to produce neurotic anxiety. I've had to struggle with this myth nearly all of my life.

As a teenager I acquired the very undesirable reputation of being a "hot head." The reputation was grounded in fact. I was frequently given to violent outbursts of temper. I was so volatile and explosive that I was almost banned from competition in interscholastic athletic events because I physically attacked an umpire in a baseball game. The memory of those experiences is always accompanied by a deep sense of shame. After my conversion to Christianity I determined to control my temper absolutely. I understood self-control to mean that there was never any just reason to be angry. That understanding was a dangerous one which didn't fully solve the problem. I learned to control my *temper*, but I failed to learn how to be in control of my *anger*. It is easy to move from a habit of explosive temper tantrums to a quiet seething rage. The quiet rage is not what God has in mind by self-control. The quiet rage may be as destructive as the explosive tantrum. The Apostle says, "Be angry, and yet do not sin; *do not let the sun go down on your anger*" (Eph. 4:26). The controlled rage has the tendency to turn into bitterness and resentment in the darkness of the night after the sun has gone down. Resentment is what comes out in an argument three weeks later in a massive dose of venom.

What does the Apostle mean when he says, "Be angry, and yet do not sin"? Obviously the Scripture is indicating that anger is not intrinsically evil. Jesus himself became angry. Paul is not saying that anger is in itself sinful but he is warning us that it may be the occasion for sin. The issue of self-control is the question of how we *deal* with anger. Violence, tantrums, bitterness, resentment and hostility (and even withdrawn silence) are all sinful responses to anger.

Perhaps the most helpful word in our vocabu-

44

lary, doing much to aid us in our quest for a godly response to irritating, annoying, and anger-producing situations, is the word "*why*." When someone offends us we can use the word "why" in two different ways. We can scream at the person or at God, whoever has provoked us, "*Why did you do that*?!" When "why" is used in this manner, it is not a question but an accusation, a challenge that only provokes more anger. But if the word "why" is used in a gentle way as a sincere inquiry into the situation it can be very helpful. The wisdom of God teaches that a "soft answer turns away wrath"—that soft answer can be effective not only in dealing with other people's anger toward us but also in turning away our own anger.

Another important key in learning self-control is by recognizing different kinds of anger and their causes. A few of those types of anger include the following.

Situational Anger

There are many different types of anger. Anger itself is a generic term containing a wide variety of species. One of the most important species is situational anger. This is the kind of anger that is provoked not by persons but by things. Its cause is impersonal, prompted by circumstances.

We all experience the painful reality of situational anger. The husband is at the office all day, and the wife has just finished vacuuming the whole house. After getting the house spic and span, the wife goes next door for a much-deserved coffee break. While she is out, the new puppy escapes from his pen, comes into the living room, knocks over a lamp, chews up the curtains, scatters paper all over the floor, and to add the final insult, re-lieves himself on the rug. The wife returns to her mutilated house, sees the mess, and buries her head in her hands, bawling her eyes out. Fifteen minutes later the husband walks in the door expect-ing a cheery greeting. What he gets is not quite cheery! He hears that it was his idea to get the puppy for the children. Why didn't he build the pen more secure? Doesn't he care about how hard she works all day? Pretty soon the wife can imagine that her husband spent six weeks with the dog in a secret obedience training school, care-fully teaching the pup the fine art of working havoc on a household.

Or turn the cards around a bit. I sometimes treat my wife as if she has an omnipotent capacity to control all the apparent contingencies of the universe. If it rains when I'm supposed to play golf, I act like it's her fault. If the plane is late or the paper didn't come, she is held responsible. Such anger is irrational, though quite common. Situational anger is misplaced or misdirected anger. In order to deal with this kind of anger two simple things need to be done: (1) Recognize situational anger for what it is. (2) Direct the anger where it belongs. The second is more difficult as it is hard to be angry with the rain. (How about the weatherman? He'll never know!)

Anger and Frustration—Disappointment

As indicated earlier, anger often grows out of frustration and/or disappointment. The anger that grows out of frustration is a frequent malady of the husband and a course of grief to the wife.

We live in a culture that is highly success-oriented. The level of competition is often fierce and few accolades are accorded those who come in second. As a result of this highly competitive atmosphere, we have become a nation of "underachievers." Failing to realize our goals leaves us in a state of disappointment and frustration. The syndrome is so bad that the unfrustrated male is a rarity. There are very few men who ever achieve all the goals they set out to achieve. When the man comes home frustrated he is very likely to be less than thoughtful and sensitive to his wife and family. That this insensitivity is born of frustration does not excuse it, but it may help the wife to understand it.

When men feel the pressure of their job they are apt to resent or belittle the "easy life" of the woman. The housewife seems to be free of competition. The family income and economic security does not depend on her work. Criticism from the wife is received like athletes receive criticism from sports writers and arm-chair quarterbacks. (Who wants to be married to Howard Cosell?) These are the feelings of resentment that often build up.

On the other hand, the wife must deal constantly with boredom and frustration. It's not very exciting or glamorous to change diapers and scrub floors. Yet these tasks must be done, over and over again. "Women's work is never done." We may call that phrase a cliché and be correct, but it has become a cliché for a reason. Too often her labor is considered unimportant and insignificant. She knows the frustration of trying to keep a house clean while everyone else in the family seems committed to a plan of systematic destruction of her work. The lack of cooperation from the rest of the family can make an excellent housekeeper look like a poor one. The work of a woman should never be taken for granted. It is usually done in order to please the husband. When the husband fails to appreciate that, a problem of resentment is likely.

Anger and Moods

Human beings have moods. Some of us resemble chameleons with our ever-changing moods. Some people are more moody than others, but all of us experience changes of emotional state. Though moods are somewhat unpredictable, there is one thing we can know for certain about them: moods always change. It is simply not humanly possible to sustain the same mood forever. The grief-stricken woman thinks she will never be able to smile again. But no matter how deep the pain of grief is, her face will not be forged into a perpetual frown. Anger can change to bitterness, but strong feelings of anger cannot last forever.

Depression can linger for long periods, but it too must give way to different feelings. If we can understand this, it is a major step toward dealing with moods. I tend to be the melancholy type, knowing frequent periods of depression. I used to turn to Kierkegaard and the modern existentialists to feed my melancholy. But when depression strikes it is comforting to know it won't last. I wonder how many suicide victims would have gone ahead with ending their lives had they waited another day. When depression hits, it is helpful to actively change your immediate environment. Go and do something different. Martin Luther conquered his depression by going outside and working in the garden. Surprisingly enough, one of the best ways to handle depression is to go to work immediately on the task you least enjoy. (The chances are your depression is caused by guilt-feelings arising out of neglect of those tasks.)

The Problem of Self-Giving

The problem of giving gifts, especially of giving yourself, was touched on in the first chapter. Let us examine it more fully as it relates to resentment. We have a general tendency to give the least expensive gifts to our partners. Least expensive in this case is not determined by monetary value but in terms of what it costs us inwardly. It is easy to give a gift you want to give. It may not be so easy to give the gift your spouse wants.

It is easy for resentment to rise when I give my wife all kinds of little gifts and she doesn't seem to appreciate them. In my mind I begin to enumerate all the things I do for her which she doesn't seem to appreciate. She doesn't seem to care. But the question is, Am I giving her the gifts she wants or am I giving the gifts I want her to want? (It is this question that is in view when I suggest that you take the test outlined at the end of chapter one.) Some of our most lavish gifts are smokescreens, mere substitutes for giving what our partners want. On whose terms are you giving yourself? Are you really giving anything of yourself? How much do your gifts cost you? These questions must be faced before any legitimate basis for resentment can be established.

Again, the essential importance of knowing your partner rises to the fore with the issue of self-giving. How can you possibly give your wife or husband what he or she needs or wants if you have no idea what those wants are? You will not discover your partner's needs by going to the Bureau of Statistics or the county courthouse. External, secondary sources will not provide you with the necessary information. This kind of personal knowledge can come through self-revelation only. There is an analogy here with our knowledge of God.

Some knowledge of God can be gained by reflecting upon the created order. We can study the trees and come to the conclusion that an intelligent being has created the universe. But God's purposes of redemption can never be learned by analyzing the component parts of a tree. The tree will tell us nothing of the intimate, personal love of the Creator. Our knowledge of redemption comes from God's self-revelation. He has taken the time not only to act in our behalf, but He has loved us enough to speak to us. No amount of unilateral study of the external aspects of creation will give us the knowledge of God that comes to us through His Word. Giving of yourself requires talking.

At the head of the list of complaints I hear from wives is the lament, "He never talks to me." If the only time you speak to someone is when they halt you and ask you a question, you are hardly showing concern for that person. Anyone can speak when spoken to. I have gotten myself in a lot of trouble over this point. If absent-mindedness is a prerequisite for being a good professor, then I qualify for the elite corps of professors of this world. I once excused myself from my wife and walked back toward the bathroom. When I didn't return, my wife came to investigate and found me undressing in the bedroom. "What in the world are you doing?" she asked. I responded, "I don't know, I just came back here to brush my teeth!" This kind of absent-mindedness could get me arrested. People complain to Vesta that they have passed me on the street and spoken to me only to have me completely ignore them. That certainly communicates a lack of concern to those who have been snubbed. Vesta knows that I frequently become involved in intense mental concentration and, consequently, tune out everything around me. She knows by now that it isn't a personal attack on her but is an occupational hazard. But a lot of people don't understand that and have felt quite hurt.

Another example is that situation first experienced by Eve. I talk with someone on the phone for an hour; and when I hang up, Vesta asks, "What did he say?" I answer, "Oh, nothing much." Or I'm gone for twelve hours and return; Vesta asks, "What did you do?" I say, "Nothing." The normal continuation of the conversation is, "Why not stay home and do nothing?" or "How can you spend hours doing nothing?" What are we saying when we tell our spouses we've done nothing? Perhaps we are saying simply that nothing unusual or nothing significant has taken place. More probably, however, we just don't want to take the time to rehearse and recapitulate what has taken place. It would cost us too much time and energy to tell our partners what they want to know. The gift is entirely too expensive. When we refuse to give the gifts that are desired, we manifest more selfishness than love.

To give the gift that is desired, we must discover what that gift is. Then, we must pay the price to give that gift rather than substitutes. Nothing is worse than to receive the gifts you do not want. The way to avoid that is to start giving the right gifts yourself.

The Problem of Maleness and Femaleness

"And God created man in his own image, in the image of God created he him; male and female he created them" (Gen. 1:27). Male and female . . . There is a difference—a difference that is much preferred to Plato's *andrygonos*. It's the differences between male and female that make love and romances so exciting. It's also the source of a multitude of problems. What does it mean to be male or female? That question is of supreme import in our contemporary culture. However that question is answered, there is at least one indisputable fact—there is a difference. The unisex movement is one movement that will never make it.

It is important in our attempt to understand the dynamics of communication in marriage that certain characteristics of our partner's behavior are not unique to our partner but represent typical male or female traits. Understanding that will help in refusing to take certain slights or insensitivities personally. When a man walks in the house and throws his coat across a chair, he is not usually manifesting an intentional insult to the wife. He is simply being typically male. Of course, not all men fail to hang their coats up when they

come home; but it is a typically male characteristic. It may be typically male, despicably male,
insensitively male, ruthlessly male, but male
nevertheless. It is not meant to be taken personally (though it is quite difficult for the woman
not to take it personally). It is simply difficult
for a husband to understand the things that are
important to a woman and difficult for a woman
to understand everything that is important to a
man.

When I come home from the golf course, I like
to sit down and go over the entire eighteen holes
with Vesta, stroke by stroke. She sits there and
listens patiently, but I can tell she's not really
paying attention. Why can't she care as much
about my golf game as I do? Well, one simple
reason is that nobody could possibly care as much
as I do about my golf game. Vesta's life just doesn't
revolve around golf. The fact that she listens at
all is a work of supererogation.

We will never be able to understand fully what
certain things mean to our spouses. All we can
do is to seek a deeper understanding than we now
have and above all understand that no personal
offense is intended. When we are offended, it is
easier to take if we know the offense was not intended.

The Problem of In-laws

In-laws can be a great benefit and help to a
marriage, but they can also be the source of a
lot of pains. Mother-in-law jokes are rooted more
in tragedy than in comedy. One of the basic biblical mandates for marriage is frequently ignored.
In the institution of marriage we read, "For this

cause a man shall leave his father and his mother, and shall cleave to his wife; and they shall become one flesh" (Gen. 2:24). Much attention has been given to the two becoming one flesh and the importance of cleaving to each other. But the first clause of the statement is virtually ignored: "A man shall *leave* his father and his mother."

What does it mean to leave your parents? It certainly does not mean that you desert them or write them off and no longer consider them important. We are not told to desert our parents, but we are called to leave them. The giving away of the bride involves more than a ceremonial ritual. A lot of parental "Indian-giving" goes on which is dangerous. The parents must allow their children to leave unless they want to lose them in a far more serious sense.

Leaving parents means first of all a geographical departure. One of the greatest mistakes a young couple can make is to live in the same house as their parents. It doesn't matter what the past relationship with the parents has been or what the economic necessities might be, it is a highly dangerous situation. Living with in-laws provokes a multitude of unnecessary tensions—not the least of those tensions is that one which involves a conflict of interests. When the husband wants his wife to do one thing and her mother another, the wife is put in a position of having to choose one over the other. No matter what she decides, somebody gets hurt. A woman going through the period of adjustment of marriage does not need that kind of problem.

In addition to the problem of conflict of interests is the problem of conflict of authority. Who is the

head of the house where there are two male figures present? Can a newly married male learn
responsible leadership when he must check every
move with his father or father-in-law? Animals
often have more sense then people. They know
enough to realize that if their young are going
to survive, they have to learn to leave their nest
and make it on their own.

Financial dependence on the in-laws can be
very destructive to the male ego and make the
husband feel less than a man. Financial aid is
one thing, but dependence is something else again.
Our whole culture is feeling the effects of radical
protests against paternalism. The first year of
marriage is crucial to the future development of
a healthy relationship. This basic insight was clear
to the people of Old Testament Israel. So highly
was the first year regarded that newly married
men were exempt from military service for the
first year of their marriage.

Leaving the parents is important for the establishing of an adult relationship with them. The
leaving represents a transition of adolescent dependence to an adult relationship that can be mu-
tually beneficial. I started "going steady" with
Vesta when I was thirteen years old (not a practice that I usually recommend). We went together
for eight years until we were finally able to get
married. I am sure that on our wedding day my
father-in-law still thought of me as the thirteen-
year-old kid who was always ringing his doorbell
and making the telephone ring in the middle of
dinner. He still represented to me the ominous
figure who gave a shrill whistle at 11 o'clock, telling me it was time to leave. In the early years

of marriage it was painful to my ego to accept the help from my in-laws that was frequently offered. But gradually things shifted to an adult relationship. My father-in-law came to realize that I was no longer thirteen, and I came to know him as a man and not merely as the father of my girl friend. I have an enormous amount of respect for that man and feel entirely free to go to him for counsel and, when necessary, even for financial assistance. I value that relationship highly and know it would never have been possible had we not once *left* and been allowed to leave. The biblical mandate to honor our parents is never abrogated in this leaving. One way to honor them is to leave them when we get married.

The Problem of Money

In my experience in marriage counseling I've discovered that two explosive issues in marriage are sex and money. How money is spent touches the entire value system of the household. Here is where conflicts of interest can be devastating. Communication in finances is an absolute must for a successful marriage. Two different people never bring exactly the same value systems into a marriage. For example, Vesta hates to spend money. She was born and raised in a household where fiscal responsibility was a priority. I kid her father about still having the first penny he ever earned. Her parents weren't the least bit selfish with their money, but they were very careful. On the other hand, my father was truly the last of the big-time spenders. For him it was always "easy come, easy go." My wife sees the same tendencies in me—and is much more concerned about the "easy go" than she is about the "easy come"!

While we were in seminary we became friends with a man who worked on the ground crew. This man didn't make much money, so he was constantly behind in his bills. We used to discuss the matter frequently, and I would ask him, "Rudy, what do you do when you get those threatening third and fourth warning notices from the bill collectors?" Rudy would smile and say, "I write them a letter and tell them that unless they start being nicer to me, I won't put their bill in the hat next month!" Vesta would go nuts being married to Rudy. She has enough trouble as it is with me.

When attitudes about money differ, it is essential to keep the lines of communication open. Both sides have to learn to bend a little for the sake of their partners. When better understanding comes, it can be a beautiful thing.

The money issue in our house reached a crisis when it came to decorating our home in Cincinnati. We had been married for over ten years and had always bought our curtains at the dime store. I had enough of that and wanted to purchase some custom curtains for the living room. Vesta was vigorously opposed. I gave Vesta my reasons, and she gave me her intuitions. Finally I won the debate, and Vesta reluctantly agreed to go along with the curtain caper. When the curtains were prepared and installed, Vesta was thrilled. Then I had a startling revelation. Vesta wanted those curtains all along. She wanted to lose the argument from the beginning. But she felt it was her moral obligation to oppose me. Then when Daddy came to visit and looked askance at the curtains, Vesta could tell him, "It was all R.C.'s idea." Learning that little bit of Vesta's psychology has paid dividends. Now when she opposes me on similar issues, I let her carry on knowing full well she wants to lose but would feel guilty if she didn't put up a fight.

She has learned a few things about my psychology of money, too. She knows that when I see some new gimmick I get all excited and want to buy it. She also knows that the more she resists me on the item the more attractive the gimmick becomes. She discovered, however, that once she says, "Go ahead and buy it," a Jekyll-Hyde transformation takes place in my psyche. As soon as I know I have the freedom to buy what I want with impunity, I shift gears into a calculating rationalist and decide not to waste the money.

I once got all excited about purchasing a second car. Vesta agreed that we could afford $500 for a second car, but not a penny more. I almost destroyed the relationship with my friend in the car business. I went to see him eleven times, trying to buy a $1,000 car for $500. I test-drove just about every car on the lot. I never did buy the car since I couldn't stand to spend the money foolishly. Vesta has come to recognize that in me and feels a lot more secure about my financial policies.

As a rule, women tend to need more financial security than men. This is not the Law of the Medes and the Persians—there is always the proverbial story of the wife and her charge account. But there are reasons why many women have a security problem with money. Unless they are working, they do not have direct control of the income situ-

58

ation. They are put in a dependent position which makes security difficult. It is important for men to realize that and be sensitive to the wife's need for financial security. On the other hand, a wife's constant nagging about the husband's financial policy can be very emasculating. It doesn't help much to have both partners insecure. When the man is super-anxious about finances, it may be a sign of a deep male-insecurity problem. If a man lacks confidence in his ability to provide for his family, that lack of confidence will have an effect on his total relationship to his family. Problems like this or of compulsive spending or constant serious indebtedness require professional counseling.

Questions for Discussion

1. Do you have problems in your relationship? How are you solving them?

2. Are you embarrassed to seek help?

3. Are your solutions to problems long-range?

4. Are you alone in your problem? Have other people successfully solved the same kind of problem? Does God offer a solution to this problem?

5. How do you deal with anger? What frustrates you? Irritates? Disappoints?

6. Give examples of situational anger you've experienced. Also *misdirected* anger.

7. How well have you achieved your goals?

8. What kind of moods do you have? What work are you behind in?

9. How easily do you give of yourself?

10. What kind of typically male or female traits do you exhibit?

11. How well do you get along with your in-laws? Do you have an adult relationship with them? Have you ever "left" them? Did you "write them off"?

12. How do you handle money? Do you agree on money? Are you financially secure? Do you feel "nagged" about money?

3
The Role of the Man and Woman in Marriage

In our lives we are involved in a multitude of tasks. We have roles to play and responsibilities to be carried out. When we have no idea what is expected of us in a given role or task, we have no way of measuring our performance. That may sound like a desirable state of freedom but in fact it is an occasion for anxiety and frustration. Only recently educators in America are declaring a failure the experiment of grading college students on a pass-fail basis. Students need to have a better idea of how well they are doing with respect to what is expected of them. Likewise in marriage we hear the pathetic statement, "I feel like a failure as a wife," or "I feel like a failure as a husband," because people have no idea of what is expected of them and how well they are performing up to those expectations. Thus it is important for a man and a woman to know what is expected of them in marriage. What is the role of the wife? What is the role of the husband?

Everyone enters into marriage with some preconceived notion of roles. We all know childbearing belongs to the woman rather than the man. But where do these other preconceived ideas come from? For the most part these notions are acquired in the home. They may be acquired via direct consciousness and analysis or by intuition. By observing our parents we formulate our ideas of the role of the man and the role of the woman. Now, when the married couple's previous home experiences match, things can go pretty smoothly. However, when roles and expectations don't correspond, tension can develop. We won't find two married people in America who agree on every single point of who is responsible for what. But it helps to explore these areas so that expectations can be as clear as possible. A helpful hint to people about to get married or who have been married for decades is to sit down and discuss with each other the roles played by their respective parents. As one counselor said to one husband, "Try to imagine your mother married to her father or your father married to her mother." In a very real way, that's exactly what you have in marriage, at least in terms of expected job description.

To see how this works out let's examine my own background. My father married his secretary. Before they were married my mother had taken care of many of the details of my father's work. That continued after they got married. Consequently I frequently hear from Vesta, "You don't want a wife, you want a secretary." When my father would go away on a business trip, my mother would cheerfully pack his suitcase for him, making sure that he had everything he would need on his trip. Now, Vesta's father did not marry his secretary. When he went away on business he packed his own bags. He preferred it that way. He knew exactly what he would need on his trip, and he wanted to make certain that everything he needed was securely packed. Now guess what happened the first time I had to go away on a business trip after we were married. Right, I asked Vesta to pack my suitcase. Her response? "Pack your own bag; you're not helpless, are you? Am I your servant?" Wow! I walked away from that one thinking, "If she loved me like my mother loved my father, she would have been happy to pack my suitcast for me." Vesta walked away thinking, "If he loved me like my father loved my mother, he wouldn't ask me to pack his suitcase." By exploring our parents' roles, we were able to avoid a lot of further conflict in these areas.

The Biblical Job Description

The New Testament does not provide a detailed list of specific responsibilities of the husband or wife. Nor do we find them noted on the back of the marriage license. The details will have to be worked out by the couple involved. To be sure, God not only ordains and institutes marriage, but He regulates it by His commandments as well. But those commandments do not tell us who is to take out the garbage or who is to pack the suitcase. However, God is not altogether silent with respect to role and responsibility. The New Testament does provide some basic principles which are essential to marriage.

The most direct commandments relative to role and responsibility are found in Paul's letter to the

Ephesians. In the fifth chapter of the epistle Paul sets down the responsibilities of the husband and the wife. He says:

> . . . be subject to one another in the fear of Christ. Wives, be subject to your own husbands, as to the Lord. For the husband is the head of the wife, as Christ also is the head of the church, He Himself being the Savior of the body. But as the church is subject to Christ, so also the wives ought to be to their husbands in everything. Husbands, love your wives, just as Christ also loved the church and gave Himself up for her; that He might sanctify her, having cleansed her by the washing of water with the word, that He might present to Himself the church in all her glory, having no spot or wrinkle or any such thing; but that she should be holy and blameless. So husbands ought also to love their own wives as their own bodies. He who loves his own wife loves himself; for no one ever hated his own flesh, but nourishes and cherishes it, just as Christ also does the church, because we are members of His body. For this cause a man shall leave his father and mother, and shall cleave to his wife; and the two shall become one flesh. This mystery is great; but I am speaking with reference to Christ and the church. Nevertheless let each individual among you also love his own wife even as himself; and let the wife see to it that she respect her husband. (Eph. 5:21-33)

Now before we plunge into an analysis of this highly controversial passage of scripture, I think it is important to place it in its proper framework in the whole epistle. These ordinances are key-noted at the beginning of the chapter. Paul begins the chapter by saying:

Therefore be imitators of God, as beloved children; and walk in love, just as Christ also loved you, and gave Himself up for us, an offering and a sacrifice to God as a fragrant aroma. (Eph. 5:1-2)

Thus the immediate context of Paul's writing is the developing of what it means to be imitators of God. Here we have a general reaffirmation of the responsibility of all men in creation. Man is created in the image of God and that entails the responsibility to reflect and mirror (as an image) the very character of God. The rest of the chapter is devoted to a detailed description of what it means to imitate God. Paul is not concerned in this chapter about providing a practical method of imitating his first-century culture; rather, he is giving concrete instructions on how a Christian can mirror and reflect the character of God to that culture.

The most important aspect of reflecting the character of God is stated in the next breath, "Walk in love, just as Christ also loved you." What follows is an explanation of what it means to walk in love. The Apostle doesn't say simply that we should walk in love and then leave it up to us to discover the content of love. He doesn't say, "Walk in love and decide for yourself what it means to walk in love." Where would we go to find out what that means? To Elmer Gantry who tells us, "Love is the morning and the evening star, the inspiration of philosophers..."? Or to Eric Segal who tells us that "love means never having to say you're sorry"? (The New Testament tells us to say we're sorry even when we don't have to.) Do we go to Hugh Hefner or Joe Namath? Why not consult the God of love who does not let love remain an abstraction or a studied ambiguity? In this chapter Paul spells out in detail what love is all about. It involves obedience and carries with it obligation. The supreme example of that love and the measuring rod of love is Christ. This chapter will appear absurd to us unless we understand these obligations against the wider context of imitating God by walking in love.

We move now to the lengthy passage quoted above, beginning with verse 21.

"And Be Subject to One Another in the Fear of Christ"

This verse does not apply merely to the discussion of marriage that follows. Rather, it is an introduction to a whole series of instructions involving a wide variety of spheres of authority. Paul deals with the authority structure of the marriage, the family (children and parents), slaves and masters, etc. The point of the statement is simple. All of us are called to positions of authority and positions of subordination—submission to authority. People have authority over animals; parents have authority over children; civil magistrates have authority over civilians, etc. No one is given ultimate or absolute authority in this world except Christ. He rules over all lesser authorities by virtue of His office as King of Kings and Lord of Lords. Thus in this passage we are taught that imitating God and walking in love involves being subject to authority. This subjection is to take place in the "fear of Christ." That is, all authority is under Christ. When we disobey lesser authorities we are guilty of disobeying Christ. You cannot serve the King and honor His authority by rebelling against His appointed governors. To say you honor the Kingdom of Christ while you disobey His authority structure is to be guilty not only of hypocrisy but cosmic treason. Submitting in the "fear of Christ" as beloved children means not a servile fear such as a prisoner has for his captor but a filial fear that a son has for his father, fear that does not wish to offend one whom he loves. Behind all of these words echoes Christ's clear statement: "If you love me, keep my commandments."

"Wives, Be Subject to Your Own Husbands, as to the Lord"

This is, undoubtedly, one of the most unpopular verses in the whole Bible. In our day, it has been the focus and target of almost unlimited criticism. For penning these words the Apostle Paul has been called a "male chauvinist," a "misogamist," and an "anti-feminist." The verse is not popular with many people who are militant for the cause of "women's liberation." I suspect that many who read this book will read no further than this point, throwing the book in the waste basket as being "more male supremacy propaganda." If you are so inclined I can only beg that you will hear Paul out before you dismiss him. He is not setting forth a case for male supremacy, nor engaging in a diatribe against women. Supression or exploitation of women is not the concern of the Apostle in this context. He is concerned with what it means to imitate God and walk in love in marriage.

When Paul calls the woman to be in subjection to her husband, he roots his argument in creation. He does not appeal to the status of women in the first-century world. He does not seek to perpetuate a concept of the inferiority of women found in the distorted cultures of ancient Greece or Rome. He is dealing with the role of woman as it is established in creation, maintained in the Old Covenant, and reaffirmed in the New Covenant. To see Paul merely echoing his culture at this point is to do violence to the text and gross insult to the Apostle. In creation, woman is not called to the subordination of a slave to a tyrant. It is the subordination of a queen to a king. In creation Adam and Eve are given dominion over the earth. Together, as God's deputy monarchs, they rule over the earth. We read in Genesis:

> And God blessed them; and God said to them, "Be fruitful and multiply, and fill the earth, and subdue it; and rule over the fish of the sea and over the birds of the sky, and over every living thing that moves on the earth." (Gen. 1:28)

Eve was created to be a queen, not a slave. Her role was that of helpmate to her husband. Throughout the narrative of creation we hear the refrain of God's benediction. God creates and then says, "That's good!" But finally the malediction comes as God observes something that is not good. The very first negative judgment we find in Holy Writ is a judgment on loneliness. God said, "It is not good for the man to be alone." So God responded to the situation of loneliness by saying, "I will make him a helper suitable for him" (Gen. 2:18). So God created woman and brought her to Adam. What did Adam say? Did he say, "A slave! Just what I always wanted"? Did he say, "Thank you, God, for this object that I can exploit at my pleasure"? God forbid. Adam was elated with this new and vital creation, exclaiming:

> This is now bone of my bones, and flesh of my
> flesh; she shall be called Woman, because she
> was taken out of Man. (Gen. 2:23)

What does it mean to be "bone of my bones and flesh of my flesh"? This is a graphic concrete Hebrew way of speaking. The Hebrew is expressing the notion of "essential unity." Man and woman are one in essence. That is to say, Adam and Eve are equal in dignity, worth, value, and glory. In essential unity there is absolutely no room for inferiority of person. The man and woman are equal in every respect except one—authority. In the job description of creation and marriage two different tasks are given to people of equal value and dignity. Only the job descriptions are different in the economy of marriage.

Perhaps the ultimate analogy that we have for the notion of essential unity with economic subordination is the classic view of the Holy Trinity. When Christians confess their faith in the Trinity they usually do it with the following formula: "The Trinity is one in essence but three in person." The three members of the Trinity are equal in glory, value, power, holiness, omnipotence, omniscience, etc. The Son is no less divine than the Father. All are fully God, being co-eternal and co-essential. The list could continue, but the idea is clear. With all this essential unity, however, in redemption there are levels of subordination. What is meant by the "economy" of redemption has nothing to do with finances or the gross heavenly product. Economy in this context has to do with *how* the plan of redemption is carried out. It deals with the division of labor of the Trinity. The Father sends the Son to redeem the world, the Son doesn't send the Father. The Holy Spirit is sent by both Father and Son, yet is equal to the Father and Son. Thus we see that in principle the notion of subordination does not carry with it the notion of inferiority. It is significant for our study that Christ willingly submitted to the Father, without a word of protest. It is precisely that willingness that we are called to imitate in submitting ourselves to authority.

When the New Testament calls wives to be in subjection to their own husbands, there is no hint or trace of female inferiority. That notion is never explicitly stated nor ever implied. When the idea is wrenched out of the Scripture, it is done so by twisted minds. What is called for is a division of labor in the economy of marriage. The role of leadership is assigned to the man and not to the woman.

In the Women's Liberation Movement we have seen a massive protest against male supremacy. Women are marching to recapture their dignity. How did they ever lose it in the first place? Because God created Adam before He created woman? Because Moses was a male chauvinist? Because Paul was a misogamist? Certainly not. The loss of female dignity came about when sinful male arrogance declared the myth that "preeminence in authority means superiority in dignity." Men arrived at the gratuitous conclusion that since God put them in charge of the home, it must have been because He knew they were intrinsically better—more wise, more intelligent, etc., and all the other nonsense men have claimed for themselves.

Unfortunately, many women in protesting their loss of dignity and taking steps to correct the problem have bought the lie that the men started. They've fallen into the trap of thinking the only way of restoring their dignity is by removing men from their position of authority and claiming that prerogative for themselves. To usurp the authority of the husband is seen by many as the only possible solution to the problem. When this happens, the authentically noble and just aspirations of Women's Lib degenerate to a Peasant's Revolt that will leave women worse off than they now are. When a good principle or institution is abused, there is always the tendency of some to destroy the principle or institution altogether—"throwing out the baby with the bath water."

Others of a less militant stripe say that they are not interested in replacing male supremacy with female supremacy—exchanging one set of oppressors for another. They want equality, not revenge. It is from this more moderate wing that we get another myth—the myth of the 50-50 marriage.

I call the idea of a 50-50 marriage a myth because it doesn't correspond to reality. No one has a 50-50 marriage, and no one ever will. A 50-50 marriage does not exist. The reason it does not exist is because it can't exist. Try to imagine a marriage with an absolutely equal distribution of authority. What happens when the husband and wife disagree on a policy decision? Suppose for example, your daughter or son wants to go to a dance. Now no external authority covers the issue. God neither commands nor prohibits your children from dancing. The civil authorities leave it up to you. Suppose the husband is convinced the child should not go to the dance and the wife is equally convinced that she should. Who decides the issue? Some might suggest at this point that these sort of issues can be dealt with in advance by agreeing that the father decides policy with respect to the son and the mother decides with respect to the daughter. Or you might agree that all social decisions are under the jurisdiction of the wife and economic decisions under the jurisdiction of the husband. That would be fine if there were an absolute line of demarcation between sociology and economics. Unfortunately that is not the case. Or perhaps the problem could be solved by agreeing in advance to submit to binding arbitration in the case of a stalemate. Pity the poor third party. He would need the collective wisdom of nine Justices of the Supreme Court. Then the problem of enforcing the decision remains as either party could still declare a wildcat strike.

What really happens when people agree to a 50-50 marriage is one of two things. Either the marriage is paralyzed by a "Mexican stand-off" or it becomes a perpetual power struggle to gain 51% or a controlling share of the authority stock. In reality, a marriage of equal distribution of authority is a marriage without leadership. Fifty-fifty authority in the final analysis means no authority. Thus the notion of a 50-50 marriage, which seems so attractive at first glance, under scrutiny reveals itself to be an euphemism for marital anarchy.

How is the submission of the wife to be carried out? According to Paul it is to be done "as to the Lord." This means several things. First is the analogy that Paul elaborates on between the man and his wife and Christ to His Church. The wife's submission to the husband is to be like the Church's submission to Christ. There is a real sense in which the husband is called to be the lord of the home. He carries the authority of Christ. Submission is to be "as to the Lord." This notion also includes the fact that in submitting to the authority of the husband, the wife is submitting at the same time to the authority of Christ.

That the husband be the head of the house is vital to a healthy marriage. Most women are well aware of that. I have yet to find a woman who would say to me that she wanted to be married to a man she could dominate. As a general rule, women want leadership from their husbands, though they do not want tyranny. What Christian woman would find it difficult to be submissive if she were married to Christ? But that's the problem—no husband is exactly like Christ. To submit to anything less than Christ is difficult in the marriage. Yet it is Christ who commands women to be submissive to their husbands, even to those who are less than Christ. In this sense Christ is the silent partner of the marriage. It is hard for a wife to submit when she disagrees with her husband. But when she knows her submission is an act of obedience to Christ, and honors Christ, it is much less difficult.

What happens if the man doesn't want to assume the responsibility of leadership and refuses to act as the head of the house, deferring all the decisions to his wife? What if the man wants his wife to be his mother rather than his wife? When this situation develops, it represents an exceedingly difficult problem. The natural tendency for the woman in such situations is to step into the void and assume the authority. This often happens even when the woman has no desire to be the leader. This tendency must be carefully avoided as it is not a good solution to the problem. The woman is free to use all of her skills and power of persuasion to help the man carry out his responsibility, but she must not assume the authority that is not hers.

This problem was brought home to me recently in a similar situation. A teenage boy came to me with a question. He explained that he was a Christian and that both of his parents clearly repudiated the Christian faith. He said to me, "Doesn't the Bible teach that the father is supposed to be the spiritual leader in the home and function as the 'priest' of the household?" I replied in the affirmative. Then he asked, "Since my father refuses to assume that responsibility, isn't it my responsibility to assume the spiritual leadership of the home?" I said to the boy, "Absolutely not. God has called you to be a Christian son, not a Christian father." The fact that his father neglected his duty in no way entitled or demanded that his son assume that role. I told the son that the best way to bear witness to Christ in his family situation was to be a model Christian son, bending over backwards to be as obedient as he could possibly be to his parents. The same principle applies to women who are married to men who neglect their duty.

Paul elaborates on the analogy of Christ and the church by saying:

> For the husband is the head of the wife, as Christ also is the head of the church, He Himself being the Savior of the body. (Eph. 5:23)

In this verse the analogy of lordship is reinforced. The Church does not have a 50-50 authority basis with Christ. Christ does not rule by referendum. The Church has no veto power or power of impeachment. The Church is not a democracy; it is a kingdom. And so is the home. Just as Christ reigns in sovereign authority over the Church, so the husband has sovereign authority over the wife. This does not mean, however, that the husband never listens to the wife's requests or petitions. Again the analogy with Christ is important. Christ hears the groans of His people. He is pleased when they bring their requests to Him and tell Him their desires. The Church is not required to walk five paces behind her groom and exist as a nonentity. Neither is the wife.

May the wife ever disobey her husband? The biblical answer to that is clear. There are times when the wife not only may disobey, but must disobey. The husband is not the only authority in the wife's life. She is also responsible to the authority of God and the authority of the state. What if the authorities conflict? Obviously the higher authority must be obeyed. A simple rule of thumb in these matters is this: A wife must disobey her husband when her husband commands her to do something God forbids or forbids her from doing something God commands. (This same principle applies when obedience to the state conflicts with obedience to God.) For example, if a husband orders his wife to murder, or steal, or commit adultery, it is the moral obligation of the wife to disobey him. Conversely, if the husband forbids his wife from attending church on Sunday morning, she should go anyway as God commands her not to forsake the assembling together with the saints for worship.

The "rule of thumb" for disobeying your husband when he commands you to do what God forbids or forbids you from doing what God commands is an easy principle to grasp but may sometimes be exceedingly difficult to apply. What about going to the church social? Does God command you to do that? What if your husband's decision makes you unhappy or oppressed? Does God command you to be happy? Does He command you to be free of oppression? Here is where the imitation of Christ touches the heart of the woman's role. To imitate Christ in the task of submission may involve a real participation in the humiliation and the suffering of Christ. There are times when the wife may disobey, but she must be very careful to insure that disobedience is done in order to obey God. It is easy to develop a false spirituality, distorting the commandments of God in such a way as to provide a spiritual subterfuge that covers the real desire to disobey the husband. Beware of the multitude of sins that people are inclined to commit in the name of some form of liberation.

The Role of the Man in Marriage

If the woman seems to have a difficult task in submitting to her husband, how much more difficult is the responsibility given the man. Not only is the man commanded to love his wife (which in earthly terms may be quite easy), but he is commanded to love her as Christ loved the Church.

Husbands, love your wives, just as Christ also

loved the church and gave Himself up for her.
(Eph. 5:25)

What does the Apostle Paul mean by the admonition, "love your wives"? On the surface it seems like the Apostle is giving some näive counsel. Picture a man going to a marriage counselor and telling him that he doesn't love his wife anymore. In fact, he says he can't stand her. She has become ugly and sloppy and is always nagging, etc. Finally the marriage counselor turns to the man and says, "What you need in order to repair your marriage is to love your wife." Some advise! What does the man do? Push a button and—bingo! He's in love again? Certainly not. The way the word "love" is normally used in our society, it is impossible to create it by an act of the will. I can't *decide* to be in love. When we talk about love, we usually do so by speaking of it in the passive voice: "It happened," or "I fell in love," or "Zing went the strings of my heart." Love in the world's view is something that happens to me, not something I can conjure by shutting my eyes, taking a deep breath, and making a decision.

This is not what Paul has in mind. In the New Testament, love is more of a verb than it is a noun. It has more to do with acting than with feeling. The call to love is not so much a call to a certain state of feeling as it is to a quality of action. When Paul says "love your wives," he is saying, "Be loving toward your wife—treat her as lovely." Do the things that are truly loving things. If the husband doesn't feel romantic towards his wife, that does not mean he can't be loving. To be sure, romance makes it a lot easier to be loving, but it is not a necessary prerequisite for fulfilling the biblical mandate.

How are husbands to love their wives? How
much love is required of the man? Paul says like
Christ loves the Church. How much does Christ
love His Church? Notice that Paul adds, "as
Christ gave himself up for her." The kind of love
Christ has for the Church is self-sacrificial love.
Consider the substance of Christ's sacrifice for
the Church. He gave everything He had, including
His life, for His bride. He withheld nothing. How
much patience does He have with His Church?
How often must He endure loss of affection and
rebellion? Is there any problem that a man could
possibly have with his wife that Christ hasn't had
with the Church? Yet He continues to love her.
What if the wife refuses to be submissive, must
the husband still love his wife? Does Christ still
love the Church? Again, if one partner refuses
to obey his responsibilities and violates his role,
that does not relieve the other person from responsibility. God does not say, "Wives be submissive
to your husbands when they are loving," or "Husbands love your wives when they are submissive."
Two wrongs still don't add up to a right. Retalia-
tion brings no honor to Christ.

One of the most important dimensions of the
analogy between Christ and the Church and a husband and his wife is the importance attached to
the wife. Christ never regards His bride with a
casual interest or considers her of secondary importance. That's no small thing. Consider the responsibilities that belong to Christ as King of the
cosmos. He is not a do-nothing king with only tit-
ular importance. He is an extremely busy king.
His is the responsibility for maintaining the entire
universe. He is not Lord merely of the Church
but of the cosmos. He must see to it that the sun

rises every day, the stars remain in their courses, earthly kingdoms rise and fall, and a host of other duties. But with this schedule, He still has time for His bride. If ever a husband had a right to neglect his wife, it is Christ. Yet the petitions from the Church are not relegated to the attention of minor angels in a heavenly bureaucracy. Christ intercedes for His people daily. He is never "away on business" and is never "too busy" for His bride. He gives himself without reservation. What woman would mind submitting herself to that kind of love?

There is a typical male syndrome that is all too easy for married men to enter. It is the syndrome of viewing the wife with steadily diminishing importance once the marriage has been achieved. Prior to the wedding, the man expends an enormous amount of energy seeking to woo and win her. He enters the courting relationship with the zeal and the dedication of an olympic-bound athlete. He gives his girl his undivided attention, making her the center of his devotion. When the marriage is achieved, our athlete turns his attention to other goals. He figures he has the romantic aspect of his life under control and now goes on to scale new heights. As soon as he is married, he begins to devote less and less time to his wife, treating her as less and less important. In the meantime the woman, being accustomed to the courting process, enters into the marriage relationship expecting it to continue. As the marriage progresses, she finds herself devoting more attention to her husband than she did before the marriage, while he is devoting less attention to her. Now she is washing his clothes, cooking his meals, making his bed, cleaning his house—maybe even packing his suitcases. At the same time, he is becoming less affectionate (though perhaps more erotic), taking her out less, and generally paying less attention to her than before the marriage.

When this syndrome is allowed to continue unchecked, a frequent result is the "affair." The affair, being popularized by novels and romanticized by Hollywood and television, has become a national epidemic. At one time in my ministry I was involved in counseling sixteen couples who were having marital problems with a third party involved. In every single counseling case I've been involved with that included an affair, I've asked the unfaithful partner the same question, "What is it that attracted you to this person?" In every single case the answer has been the same in so many words, "He made me feel like a woman," or "She made me feel like a man again." It's easy to make a woman feel like a woman during courtship. It's not so easy to do it in marriage. It simply cannot be done if the wife is regarded as being of secondary importance. When Paul speaks of the necessity of the husband giving himself to the wife as Christ gave himself to the Church, he is touching the very heart of marriage.

There are certain kinds of men who are particularly vulnerable to wife-neglect. Men involved in public service can easily delude themselves into thinking their work is more important than their wives. Clergymen and doctors must especially be wary of this as they are always on call to "duty."

Though it can never be a substitute for daily

concern and attention for the wife, the annual honeymoon can be a great boon to a growing marriage. After ten years without one and then finally experiencing the opportunity of being away together for a week, Vesta and I resolved never to go through another year without a honeymoon. We go away without the children, and we can then give our undivided attention to each other. I've asked many couples if they ever go away like this, and they often respond in the negative. When I ask why, they invariably answer, "We can't afford it." Yet these people have two cars, a color TV, etc. I would love to have two cars, but I can't afford that and a honeymoon too. Vesta and I find these honeymoons so meaningful that they represent a necessity and not a luxury in our budget.

Paul goes on to elaborate on the analogy of Christ and the Church by calling attention to the purpose of Christ's sacrificial self-giving:

> That He might sanctify her, having cleansed her by the washing of water with the word, that He might present to Himself the church in all her glory, having no spot or wrinkle or any such thing; but that she should be holy and blameless. (Eph. 5:26)

Christ's goal is to present His bride in "all her glory." Why does He want to do that? Christ has intrinsic glory—the glory of the only begotten Son of God. He certainly doesn't need any more glory. The Church has no intrinsic glory. Any glory the Church has is derived. It gains its glory exclusively from Christ. Christ doesn't need the Church, yet His passionate concern is that His bride possess the fullness of glory. The Latin equivalent for the Greek word for glory is *dignitas*. When the New Testament speaks of the Church's glory, it is speaking of its dignity. By analogy, the husband is called to give himself to the purpose of establishing his wife in the fullness of dignity. When he uses his authority to destroy his wife's dignity, he becomes the direct antithesis of Christ. He mirrors not Christ but the Antichrist.

After marriage the biggest single influence on the development of the wife's personality and character is the husband. When a man comes to me and complains about his wife and says, "She's changed since we got married," I immediately respond by asking, "Who do you suppose changed her?" There is a very real sense in which the wife a man has is the wife he has produced. If he has a monster, maybe he ought to examine his own nature.

In the above-mentioned passage, it is clear that the husband is called to be the priest of his home. The man is responsible for the spiritual well-being of his wife. Her sanctification is his responsibility. There is probably no male task that has been more neglected in our society than this one. The Christian Church in America is becoming a feminine organization. Count the heads in your church on Sunday morning and see how many more women are present than men. My adult education classes are filled with women whose husbands are home in bed or at the golf course on Sunday morning. While the wives are growing spiritually, the husbands are going to seed. I get a lot of static from men whose wives are bugging them to get more involved in the church. The man should know more about the things of God than his wife and certainly more than his children. He should be the primary teacher and prime example for his wife. This is an awesome responsibility—a responsibility for which every husband will be held accountable. The priestly role of the husband is not optional, but mandatory.

In seeking the sanctification of the Church, there is a sense in which Christ seeks to change His wife. So the husband is called to change his wife. But that change is not supposed to ruin her. The change is to be toward a higher conformity to the image of Christ. We are to seek to present our wives to Christ as holy and blameless, being without spot or wrinkle!

Paul goes on to say:

> So husbands ought also to love their own wives as their own bodies. He who loves his own wife loves himself; for no one ever hated his own flesh, but nourishes and cherishes it, just as Christ also does the church, because we are members of His body. (Eph. 5:28-30)

How much do you love your body? How much time do you spend trying to make it look nice and feel good? Oh, what we go through for the sake of our bodies! Right this minute, as I am penning these lines, I am about to go crazy for the sake of my body. I am trying to lose twenty pounds by means of Dr. Atkins Diet Revolution. I'm "purple" and the pounds are beginning to go. But for a carbohydrate addict this diet is not my idea of fun. I'd give my kingdom for a loaf of bread or a baked potato!

What do you do when someone attacks your body? I know I become defensive when someone tries to harm me. I'm always a little amused and even more annoyed when someone attacks me verbally; and as soon as I begin to reply the person says, "Don't get defensive!" It's like Hitler mobilizing his panzer division for a blitzkrieg and telling the Polish Chief of State not to get defensive. The Apostle's point is clear. Husbands are called to love their wives as their own bodies. Does that not imply that the husband will do everything in his power to protect and defend his wife from any possible harm? He is to be her knight in shining armor, guarding her in body, mind, and soul.

Finally, the husband is called to nourish and cherish his wife. Do you cherish your wife? That is to say, do you put a high value on her? Do you enjoy the advances of other women or do you regard them as a threat to your cherished marriage?

I began my professional teaching career at age 26. Being a college professor who deals with girls only a few years younger can be very hazardous. For many young women there is a certain charisma attached to the professor, especially if he is young. Some make it a point of sorority honor to try to seduce these men. I remember one young thing who behaved in a very seductive way, both in clothing and manner. After one examination, she came to my desk to turn in her paper, and in a super-sultry voice said to me, "I have a very difficult time expressing myself with *words*, Mr. Sproul." I turned red and said, "Unfortunately, Miss ———, words are all that count on this exam." Though I was flattered and my ego was titillated, I soon learned that indulging my ego to such flattery could be a serious threat to my marriage. If that sort of thing happens now, a little defense button rings inside of me, and I feel insulted rather than flattered because my cherished marriage is at stake.

Recently I read about the rise in the divorce statistic in America. In the same article there were published the results of a poll taken among couples who were not divorced. The poll dealt with one question, "If you had it to do over again, would you marry the person you're married to now?" The results of the poll were staggering. A vast majority of the people answered "no." How much do they cherish their partners? While driving one day, I asked myself the same question, adding one new dimension. I asked the question, "If I could be married to any woman in the world, whom would I like to be married to?" In an instant, without hesitation, the answer came—Vesta. What a thrill to know that in the privacy of my own soul I could say that. My wife submits to my authority. She is no slave. She is feisty and spirited, every inch a woman. She is a helpmate, and I wouldn't trade her for anyone. She knows she is cherished.

What kind of role do you play in your marriage? Does your role imitate God? Do you walk in love? If you do, you have a happy marriage.

Questions for Discussion

1. What roles do you fulfill in the home?
2. What roles did your parents fulfill?
3. Does Christ have the authority to regulate your role?
4. Does subordination mean inferiority?
5. What is a helpmate?

6. Do you want a 50-50 marriage?

7. Do you want male "leadership" in the home? Is it there?

8. When can a wife disobey her husband?

9. What is the difference between biblical love and Hollywood love?

10. What does it mean for a husband to "give himself" to his wife?

11. Why do people have affairs?

12. What makes you feel like a man? a woman?

13. How often do you go away together? How can you manage it more often?

14. Who is the spiritual leader in your home?

15. What does it mean to "cherish" your spouse?

4
Communication and Sex

If money is *one* of the main problem areas of marriage, sex is far and away the number one problem. It is axiomatic that if this dimension of marriage is not healthy, there is little chance that the marriage as a whole will be happy. Consequently, it is imperative that a conscious effort be made to establish a sound basis for sexual communication in marriage.

As God regulates the institution of marriage, that regulation certainly applies to the sexual dimension as well as to the other aspects. However, the Bible does not provide us with a sex manual including detailed instructions with regard to sex. We cannot turn to the Scriptures to find out everything we always wanted to know about sex but were afraid to ask. Many thinkers today have concluded that we can learn virtually nothing about sex from the Bible because it is so hopelessly out of date. The opinion reigns in many circles that the biblical sex ethic merely reflects the normal, customary attitudes and taboos of primitive, unenlightened men. The sex ethic is regarded as a reflection of ancient culture and nothing more. I will not be taking that approach in the following discussion. I am proceeding from the premise that the biblical ethic represents nothing less than the revelation of God himself and carries the force of divine authority. Not only does it express divine authority, however, but it manifests the wisdom of God himself.

My primary concern in this chapter is to deal with the question of sex within the context of marriage. Hence I will touch only lightly on the questions of premarital and extramarital sex. If anything is clear in both Old and New Testaments, it is the strict prohibitions concerning pre- and extra-marital sex. In the Old Testament the prohibition of adultery is included in the Ten Commandments and is a capital offense. In the New Testament the death penalty for adultery is abrogated, but adultery is still regarded as a gross and heinous sin. It is a sin that carries with it the threat of excommunication from the Body of Christ and the loss of the Kingdom of Heaven. However, it is not the unforgivable sin. That adultery can be forgiven is clearly seen in the dealing of Jesus with the woman caught in adultery and His dealing with Mary Magdalene. That forgiveness, however, does not come without repentance. Jesus freely forgives the woman in adultery and does not condemn her, but He adds, "Go and sin no more." Illicit sexual practices are linked with the sin of idolatry and bring defilement to the Christian community. (See 1 Cor. 6, 2 Cor. 12, and 1 Thess. 4.)

The question of premarital sex is dealt with biblically in terms of fornication. The ethic is so clear that Paul exclaims to his readers, "Let not fornication be once named among you as befitting saints" (Eph. 5:3). That Paul didn't even want to hear of a single case of fornication in the church speaks of the strong attitude that prevailed in the early church about premarital sex.

Because the biblical sex-ethic is stated so strictly and the penalties so severe, many have come to the erroneous conclusion that God regards sex as intrinsically evil. Frequently in the history of the Church we have heard the notion expounded that sex within marriage is a necessary evil, tolerated by God for the sake of procreation. But this viewpoint represents a radical distortion of the biblical view of sex. Indeed, God gives strong prohibitions concerning the use of sex outside the context of marriage, but those prohibitions do not apply within the context of marriage. Sex is not regarded as being evil in itself, but only when found outside the institution of marriage.

Theologians have been able to trace the influences on the development of the Church that have come not from the Scriptures but from pagan sources. For example, several varieties of Neo-Platonic philosophy have made their impact at different periods of the Church's growth. Within Neo-Platonism, the physical world is regarded as being at best an imperfect copy of the spiritual world. Consequently anything of a physical nature is imperfect. From this basic concept, theories degenerated to the point that anything of a physical character was considered to be intrinsically evil. Through the added influence of Manichaeanism, men sought to purify their souls from sin by total abstinence from sex, rigorous fasting, and flagellation of the body. Deeply imbedded in the Roman Catholic tradition is the idea that people sin at least venially when they engage in sexual intercourse within marriage. In the great debate over artificial means of birth control that has rocked the Church at her foundations in our time, the question of whether or not sexual relations can properly be enjoyed without a view toward procreation has been central. The question of the pleasure of sex has been very much at issue.

Added to the intrusion of pagan views of sex into the church has been the serious misunderstanding of Paul's frequent reference to the welfare of the body and the spirit. This was seen as a conflict between physical desires and the higher inclinations of the soul. Though this warfare may indeed involve such a conflict, Paul's thinking cannot be reduced to that. In the conflict between flesh and spirit, Paul is dealing with a qualitative struggle that exists between sin and righteousness. When the Christian becomes quickened by the Holy Spirit and is regenerated, that regeneration does not mean the destruction of the physical aspect of life. Man's physical nature is not to be destroyed but redeemed.

The Old Testament bears witness to the fact that the physical universe carries the benediction of God. God creates physical things and calls them good. It was God who invented sex, and He did not denounce it as an intrinsic evil or a necessary evil. The New Testament also bears witness to God's benediction of the physical dimension of life. At the heart of Jesus' mandate is the passionate concern for the physical well-being of man. He is concerned about clothes, about food, shelter, etc. The ultimate hope of the Christian is the resurrection of his own body. Contrary to the Greek notion of redemption *from* the prison-house of the body is the New Testament hope of the redemption *of* the body.

For years commentators of the Old Testament have interpreted the Song of Solomon as an allegory of Christ and the Church. That interpretation was not motivated merely by literary considerations. All too often the ruling factor was the fact that the commentator simply could not conceive of God inspiring such a blatantly erotic love song unless it was to be interpreted allegorically. I take the position with respect to the Song of Solomon that God the Holy Spirit did in fact inspire it as a love song. It is a love song that celebrates the holy situation of sexual love and the sanctity of the physical aspects of marriage. Listen to the words of the song:

> Behold, you are beautiful, my love, behold you are beautiful! Your eyes are doves behind your veil. Your hair is like a flock of goats, moving down the slopes of Gilead . . . Your lips are like a scarlet thread, and your mouth is lovely . . . Your two breasts are like two fawns, twins of a gazelle, that feed among the lilies . . . How sweet is your love, my sister, my bride! how much better is your love than wine, and the fragrance of your oils than any spice! Your lips distil nectar, my bride; honey and milk are under your tongue; the scent of your garments is like the scent of Lebanon. A garden locked is my sister, my bride, a garden locked, a fountain sealed. (Song of Sol. 4, RSV)

Here we have a high use of imagery in the celebration of the physical beauty of the bride. Even the breasts are mentioned as part of that beauty. Even if the song were to be interpreted allegorically, we would still have to face the erotic character of the images employed. It is hard to imagine that the Holy Spirit would sanctify such images if they carried an intrinsically negative or evil connotation.

Further confusion of the biblical attitude toward sex in marriage results from improper inferences drawn from Paul's teaching on celibacy. In his letter to the Corinthians, he says:

> I wish that all were as I myself am. But each has his own special gift from God, one of one kind and one of another. To the unmarried and the widows I say that it is well for them to remain single as I do. But if they cannot exercise self-control, they should marry. For it is better to marry than to be aflame with passion. (1 Cor. 7:7-8, RSV)

Here Paul places a high value on celibacy and expresses his own wish that more people would take that option. However, two distortions frequently attend the reading of this text. The first is that distortion that reads into Paul's words a negative view of marriage. It is important to note that Paul's comparison between marriage and celibacy is not a contrast between the good and the bad, but a comparison between the good and the better. He neither states nor implies that it is bad to be married. He says later, "But if you marry, you do not sin, and if a girl marries she does not sin" (1 Cor. 7:28). He concludes this section of his epistle by saying, "So that he who marries his betrothed does well; and he who refrains from marriage does well" (7:38). Paul does not say that he who marries his betrothed does bad. The reason Paul gives for his preference of celibacy is the urgency of the mission of the Church and not the intrinsic evil of sex.

The second common distortion of the above-mentioned passage is the interpretation of Paul's words, "It is better to marry than to burn." Many have read into the statement a warning about burning in hell. But as the total context plainly reveals, Paul is not talking about future punishment in hell but the very clear and present danger of the single person being consumed by the burning flames of the sex drive. He tells such people to get married, realizing that though it is forbidden to give vent to that passion outside of marriage, it is perfectly all right to fulfill that drive within marriage.

Let the preceding examples suffice to show that sex is permitted in marriage. However, we must not stop at that point. If we examine the New Testament closely, we will discover something that has often been obscured; we will discover that sex is not only permitted in marriage, it is commanded. That God not only permits but commands sexual relations in marriage should put to rest forever any notions of the intrinsic evil of sex. God simply does not command us to do that which is intrinsically evil.

In the same epistle where Paul discusses celibacy, he sets down basic principles and obligations concerning sex in marriage. He writes:

> The husband should give to his wife her conjugal rights, and likewise the wife to her husband. For the wife does not rule over her own

body, but the husband does; likewise the husband does not rule over his own body, but the wife does. Do not refuse one another except perhaps by agreement for a season, that you may devote yourselves to prayer; but then come together again, lest Satan tempt you through lack of self-control. (1 Cor. 7:3-5, RSV)

Here Paul describes sexual relations as a duty. The married couple have a sexual responsibility to each other. In very few places does the Bible speak of human rights. Normally the Bible is more concerned about teaching us our obligations than our rights. But here is one of those places where a right is mentioned—it is the right of the husband and the wife to each other's bodies. Here also is one place where the man and the woman have equal authority in marriage. The wife has authority over the husband's body and the husband has authority over the wife's body in the sexual context. Imagine that! I wonder how many marital problems would be solved if this one principle were consistently maintained.

Abstinence from sex is allowed in marriage, but only under specific conditions. The conditions involve, first, mutual consent. The wife or husband is not permitted to use one's body as a weapon or instrument of punishment. One partner cannot "shut off" the other as a means to win an argument. This is a serious violation of God's command. The second condition is that the abstinence be temporary and not permanent. It is to be "for a season." You cannot flee the sexual obligation by deciding on a permanent prayer meeting. The third condition is that the abstinence be for a specific purpose. The implication of the text is that the purpose ought not to be trivial. The final condition is that the couple come back together lest they fall into temptation. Thus we have in this text the clear teaching that sex is a fundamental obligation of marriage. That obligation must not be violated or abused if the marriage is to be healthy.

Basic Problems of Sex Within Marriage

There are a host of problems of a sexual nature that can plague a marriage. I will not endeavor to deal with all of them, but rather with those that occur most frequently. At or near the top of the list is the problem of female frigidity.

Female Frigidity

There is no simple definition for female frigidity, as there are different forms and levels of it. But in all of its manifestations, frigidity involves a kind of sexual paralysis. In this paralysis the woman is inhibited from full and free expression of her sexuality. The term "frigid" stems from the idea of being frozen or locked in a state of nonresponse. Also the word carries the implication of being cold rather than burning with passion. There are several factors that can cause or contribute to frigidity.

The Factor of Guilt. Guilt can be a strong inhibiting factor in sexual expression. There can be many causes for the presence of guilt. For many women the transition from a place where sex is strictly forbidden to where it is not only permitted but commanded involves a difficult adjustment. Overnight she is thrust into a totally new moral climate for sex. It is not easy for her to shift gears psychologically. The woman has a difficult time really believing that sex is all right. She harbors the suspicion that it is sinful or dirty.

On many occasions I have had women come to me for counseling and tell me frankly that their problem is that they are frigid. But I have detected a slight note of pride in their voices as they tell me that. Deep within themselves they are proud that they are keeping themselves relatively undefiled. I usually ask such women, "Have you repented of your frigidity?" They look at me in shocked disbelief, confirming my suspicion that the element of pride is involved. The idea of repentance had never entered their minds, though they broached the subject of their frigidity in an attitude of "confession." Of course I don't mean to suggest that all forms of frigidity are manifestations of sin that require repentance. Rather, in these cases I mention it partly as shock therapy. I would not advise the husband to tell his wife to repent if she is frigid. What is usually needed is some in-depth education (indeed, re-education) of the woman that she might fully and finally grasp the fact that sex within marriage is not wrong. (That is mainly why I have spent so much time already laboring the point in this chapter.) It would probably be very difficult for the woman to receive this education from her husband. Is it any wonder that the wife is not quick to respond to her husband's statements about what the Bible says? The man may have a credibility gap with his wife at the level of sex ethics. She could respond to his "teaching" by saying, "I know you, you have a vested interest in this and you'll appeal to anything to support it, even the Word of God." The poor

woman probably has a history of moral crises provoked by her husband trying to convince her that
sex was all right before their marriage. The husband needs to be very patient with his wife at
this point, particularly if she is struggling with
her husband's loss of credibility for legitimate reasons.

Another form of guilt paralysis is that related
to unresolved guilt feelings that go back to premarital days. Many women carry an enormous
burden of guilt into marriage that festers for years.
Women seem to have a greater capacity for guilt
endurance than men when it comes to sex. One
question I frequently ask men who complain to
me about their wives' frigidity is, "Did you have
sexual relations with your wife before you were
married?" I go on to explain that it is not necessary to answer the question, but the answer to
the question may be helpful. In every case where
I have asked this question, the man has responded
in the affirmative. Then I ask the next question:
"Would you say that your wife was more or less
responsive to you sexually before you were married?" Again, in every case where I have asked
this question, the man has replied quite emphatically that his wife was indeed more responsive
before they were married. Then they usually look
at me with a puzzled glance and say, "How did
you know that?" The answer is that it is a rather
common phenomenon. There can be many plau-
sible explanations for the man's evaluation. It may
be simply that his memory is not too good and
he's letting his nostalgia for the good old days cloud
the evaluation of his wife's present performance.
It could be, however, that his memory is excellent

and that his wife was in fact more responsive before marriage. Why? Perhaps it was because sex was a novelty for her that now has grown dull. Perhaps the fact that sex was forbidden made it more exciting for her. Or it could be for a host of other reasons. But one explanation should be given weighty consideration. Perhaps the woman feels so guilty about her loss of virginity before marriage that she is now suffering the paralyzing effects of that guilt.

Other factors complicate the problem of frigidity. For example, the woman may experience guilt and then feel resentment toward the husband, unconsciously punishing him by withholding herself from complete involvement. Or the woman may have difficulty in giving herself to the man who once offended her (even if *she* encouraged him to sleep with her). Another factor may be that the woman felt "bound" to the man once she slept with him, and she would not have married him if they had not had intercourse. The woman may feel "trapped" in marriage.

The remedy for this kind of guilt problem will never be found by telling the woman that her guilt feelings are unrealistic and that she has nothing to feel guilty about. Within the space of one week I had two different college girls come to me with a guilt problem. Both were seniors; both were engaged to be married when school was out; both were deeply committed Christians; and both told me virtually the same story. Each girl confessed to me that she was involved in sexual intercourse with her fiance. Each experienced a profound sense of guilt about it. Both went to see a clergyman for counsel. In both cases the clergyman told the girls that they were "okay." He explained to them that they had done nothing wrong. They were not promiscuous and had done what they did in a context of love and commitment. It was merely a normal expression of that love which, in fact, would be helpful in their adjustment to marriage. He went on to explain that the reason they felt guilty was because they had been victimized by the cultural myth of sexual prohibition. He explained that the myth was the legacy of our Puritan ancestors and the Victorian Era. In a word, the minister dealt with the girls' guilt by telling them that they were not guilty. They both then said the same thing to me, "But, Mr. Sproul, I still feel guilty." I replied, "Perhaps the reason you fell guilty is because you are guilty. The answer to your guilt problem is not rationalization, nor self-justification, but forgiveness." The price of forgiveness is repentance. Without it there is no forgiveness and no relief from the reality of guilt.

What do you do with the person who says, "I've asked God to forgive me about this, but I still feel guilty." I hear that statement over and over again. I usually say to these people, "If you still feel guilty, then pray to God again; but this time don't ask Him to forgive you for the sin that is haunting you; rather, ask Him to forgive you for insulting His integrity by refusing to accept His forgiveness. Who are you to refuse to forgive yourself when God has forgiven you? When God promises to forgive His people when they repent, He is not playing games. If He says He will forgive you, then He will forgive you. And if God forgives you, you are forgiven." It is often a very difficult thing to accept the grace of God. Our human arrogance makes us desire to atone for our own sins or to "make it up to God" with works of super-righteousness. But the fact of the matter is that we can't make it up to God. We are "debtors who cannot pay." That's what justification by faith is all about.

The Factor of Fear. Female frigidity can be caused not only by guilt but by fear as well. Again several different varieties of fear may be involved with the problem. Probably the most formidable fear is the fear of physical or emotional injury. If the husband is rough or insensitive in his sexual technique, this can easily provoke feelings of fear in which the woman becomes "frozen" with terror. A woman might want strong leadership in her marriage, but she usually wants that strength to be tempered with tenderness. The only remedy for this problem is for the husband to change. If he causes physical or verbal abuse during sex, then that abuse simply has to stop.

Many husbands who are rough with their wives do not intend to be rough. They may simply be weak in their ability to control their passion or, perhaps even more likely, they do not realize their own strength. Men can hurt women unintentionally simply out of ignorance. A typical problem with husbands is a woeful ignorance of the basic physiology of sex; women usually have a greater understanding of this dimension. Perhaps this is because men are less inclined to seek help in understanding the physiological dimensions of sex than women. Women seem to be less embarrassed about discussing these matters with their family doctor or studying educational material on the subject.

The male likes to think that he knows all there is to know about sex. He is too proud to admit his real ignorance. Graffiti may be an interesting tool for insight into some aspects of a culture, but it is not a very good guide to the physiology of sex.

Another kind of fear that can contribute to frigidity is the fear of failure. There are many women who look at themselves as sexual underachievers and thus feal inadequate as sex partners. This sense of inadequacy may be related to her husband's spoken or implied criticisms of her performance. It may also come from an overdose of cultural mythology. In novels, films, TV and other media the image of the "sensuous woman" is being drummed into our minds. Who can perform up to "J's" standards? Who can compete with the goddesses of stage and screen? In the fifties the feminine status symbol was the vaginal orgasm. In the sixties the status symbol became multiple orgasm. The debate sounded like the arguments men had over how many shaves they could get out of a single razor blade when stainless steel blades first came out. This super-standard of sensuality is often very threatening to men as well. They compare their sex performance to the national average. Forget about these cultural fetishes. You are not called to compete with myths in the marriage bed. (To be sure, if you are having sexual relationships with your husband once every six months or four times a day seven days a week, then maybe you *ought* to look at the national average.) You are under no obligation to satisfy the Gallup pollster. You are called to satisfy your husband. You have only one standard to meet.

Keep your eye on that and forget the superstars of sex. Sometimes just recognizing that you are being paralyzed by a fear of failure will help you to overcome the problem. One thing is certain, no matter how well or how poorly you perform now, it could be worse and it could be better. There are ways to make it better. You can still grow in a nonthreatening way.

Another form of fear comes from a threat of exposure or of discovery. This kind of fear is accentuated when there are children in the house or when the couple is living in close quarters. Privacy is a very important ingredient of intimacy. A very practical and inexpensive solution to this problem may be a lock on the bedroom door. For a small sum of money and minimum amount of labor the lock can provide a wealth of benefits. It never ceases to amaze me that building contractors can be so oblivious to the average homeowners' basic needs for privacy. A lock on the bathroom door is standard equipment, but the bedroom door is often overlooked in the building plans.

Many other fears could be elucidated, such as fear of pregnancy or its effects. The woman who is prone to miscarriage may be very reluctant to risk pregnancy even though she may have a deep desire for children. The emotional trauma of miscarriage may overrule the desire for childbearing. More serious cases of frigidity may require medical and psychological therapy.

At the practical level there are two essential ingredients to overcoming frigidity: patience and hard work. They need to come in large doses. But frigidity can be overcome, and when it is the marriage is refreshed and renewed.

Male Impotency

As in the case of female frigidity, impotency can be found in many forms and levels of intensity. Basically, impotency is the lack of ability to adequately perform sexually. Usually impotency is related to the inability to have or sustain an erection or the problem of premature ejaculation. In diagnosing a problem of impotency, the duration of the love-making process is relevant. If the entire process is completed in five or ten minutes, this is probably a sign of impotency in the form of premature ejaculation. If the other extreme is the case (well over an hour), then the erection problem is probably in evidence. As in the case of female frigidity many of the same causes are operative. Guilt, fear, and ignorance are the three main culprits here. A review of the causes of the remedies for frigidity would be helpful.

Perhaps the dominant factor in male impotency is insecurity. What few women seem to realize but desperately need to realize is that the male ego is one of the most fragile instruments of God's creation. Though men have a tendency to put on a great act of virility and ostentatious display of their masculine strength, underneath all the bravado they are very vulnerable to sexual insecurity. The theory is that men who are conditioned to live in a highly competitive atmosphere feel this competition no less in the sexual arena.

The male who gains a reputation for being a Don Juan or a lady-killer may be a very insecure man. He may be driven sexually not by biological or physiological impulses but by psychological ones. He has a psychological need to have many "conquests" so he can convince himself that he is a man. This is a very subtle form of impotency.

Most men would like to think that they are sexually attractive. But our culture screams to the man that though the female figure is beautiful, the male figure is not. Only recently with the advent of *Playgirl Magazine* has the male nude been in vogue. The nude female has a provocative image. The nude male lacks that image. The man would like to think that his wife is as easily and quickly aroused by the sight of his body as he is by hers. Here the wife can be helpful to the impotent male by seeking to understand the dynamics of his ego and helping him to gain sexual security. Don't be fooled by an apparent air of confidence that your husband presents. He may be highly successful at his job. His co-workers may consider him the paragon of masculinity. He may be a king on the corporate ladder with a track record of successes behind him. Yet he may be a sniveling coward in the bedroom. Sometimes the main reason he is so successful in the competitive world of males is because he is desperately trying to prove his manhood that is seriously threatened by his inadequacy at home.

A frequent complaint of wives is that their husbands often go too quickly through intercourse. If the woman is frigid she may be grateful to get it over with in the shortest possible time. However, many women feel cheated and used by the husband. Deep resentment might manifest itself at this point. The woman feels exploited and robbed. Chances are, however, the man is not motivated by a desire to "use" the woman but by fear. The idea of becoming more deeply involved is terrifying to him, lacking confidence in his ability to perform in a sustained situation. As in the case of female frigidity, a lot of time and patience and understanding, plus hard work, are all necessary to overcome these problems.

What Is Permitted in Sex?

The question of the limits of sexual pleasure is one that is frequently raised by Christians. The Bible does not provide us with a detailed list of prohibitions in this area. Certain things, however, are clearly prohibited. Adultery or whatever inclines toward adultery is forbidden. Group sex would clearly be a form of adultery. Bestiality (sexual relations with animals) is also strongly forbidden. Homosexual acts are also repudiated by Scripture. A wide variety of questions are left, however, as to what is permissible between husband and wife. As I read the Bible it seems to me that God has given great freedom in this area. I take the position that as long as the positive principles of conjugal love are maintained, the married couple has a great deal of latitude.

What about sex manuals? Should we consult them to help us over our sexual problems? Basically sex manuals come in three forms. There are the technical books written by medical professionals which provide information in clinical terms. There are semi-popular manuals which seek to promote sound sexual education in everyday language that people can easily understand. The third type is the crass sex manual sold in porno shops that is designed more to arouse than to educate. Obviously the latter type is of little educational value. Much help can be gleaned from the technical type though it may be difficult for the layman to read and understand. The semi-popular type (which is experiencing a bonanza on the best-selling lists) may also be helpful. But it is frequently necessary to read these books "with a comb." Attitudes toward sexual ethics in these books are often on a collision course with Christianity. Some are openly hostile to Christianity, blaming the influence of the Christian faith for a host of sexual neuroses. In many of these books Christianity is seen as the great inhibitor of sexual liberation and maturity. The medical-technical books may be even more subtle in their posture against the Christian ethic.

Running through the popular sex manuals is the principle of what I call statistical morality. Ethical judgments are made on the basis of what is "normal." The normal is determined by statistical analysis. This is the basic approach of humanism as a philosophy. What is most human is considered good. The human is often determined by the "normal." Whatever deviates from normal human behavior is then judged to be detrimental to human fulfillment. Thus statistical surveys like those presented by Kinsey, Chapman, or Masters and Johnson become standards for ethical decisions. It's the old argument of "everybody is doing it." If it can be shown that the majority of people practice premarital sex, then it is considered normal and therefore all right. Or if a primitive tribe of Fiji Islanders regularly practice sexual relations with animals without any immediate apparent ill effects, the conclusion might be that such acts are natural and are merely excluded from civilization by cultural whim.

The Christian faces many problems with statistical moralty. In the first place, he is committed to the fact of man's fall into sin. What seems to be normal may be only an expression of human corruption. In the second place the Christian is called to a life of nonconformity. He is called to be above normal in comparison to the standards of this world. He is not to conform to, but transform, the statistical norm. Finally, a consistent application of statistical morality would create a shambles of ethics. If we can show that every human being practices lying at one time or another, we could conclude that dishonesty is normal and therefore good.

I once asked a class of students if any of them cheated in their other courses. I was shocked by the response (though I shouldn't have been). Not only did a majority of the students admit that they cheated, but every single person in the class admitted to it. This represented a statistic of 100 percent. (They all were honest enough to admit their dishonesty.) If I followed the conclusions of statistical morality, perhaps I should have invited the students in my class to cheat their heads off.

The Christian who seeks to follow the ethic of the New Testament is often brought into conflict with opinions and institutions of his culture. I have experienced a great deal of conflict with psychiatrists. For years I bent over backwards to cooperate with the men of that profession. I have a great deal of respect for the educational requirements of the field. I know of no other field that requires more academic work to become a professional than the field of psychiatry. As far as I know, the two professional occupations that require the most education in our culture are those of the psychiatrist and the theologian. My own profession involved a requirement of eleven years of higher education. That represents an enormous investment of scholarship. Hence I do not take the opinions of psychiatrists lightly. The conflict usually comes not in the area of diagnosis or in questions of medical treatment but in the areas of ethics and guilt.

When a woman comes to me and tells me that her psychiatrist has recommended that she divorce her husband because she needs to learn how to live freely in creative self-expression, I experience conflict. When psychiatrists tell people they are not really guilty when they have violated the laws of God, I have conflict. When one deals with guilt at any level, the problem is indeed a psychological one, but it is also a deeply theological problem. The study of theology is not the study of God in isolation from other concerns. It involves the study of God in relation to man. Thus our understanding of man, his values, his needs, his aspirations, etc., are all related to our understanding of God. As Doestoevsky said, "If there is no God, all things are permitted." But if there is a God and His name is Yahweh and His Son is Jesus, then not all things are permitted, least of all selfishness. The Christian must be aware of this if he is to derive benefit from semi-popular sex manuals.

Within the context of marriage, variety and creativity are important dimension. There is no reason in the world why our love-making should be dull or boring. There is no law that says sex must be enjoyed at the same time, at the same place, in the same way every time. There *is* a law that says it must be with the same partner. But beyond that there is much room for variety and creativity. Gardening is not too much fun when we grow the same kind of flower in the same spot all the time. Part of the knowing process that is involved in marriage can be vastly enriched by new explorations and new experiences acheived together. This requires some thought and study— "doing what comes naturally" is a poor educational method.

The second week of our honeymoon was spent at the home of my uncle. After returning from the first week he looked at me with a sly grin on his face and said, "Well, how do you like it?" I said, "Terrific!" Then he said, "You don't know what it is all about yet; just wait fifteen years." I looked at his middle-age paunch and thought to myself, "What does this old codger know that I don't know?" I'm just beginning to find out what the old man was talking about. So can you.

Questions for Discussion

1. What does God say about sex outside of marriage?

2. Is sex within marriage sin?

3. What does it mean to be "frigid"?

4. What are some causes for frigidity?

5. Do you have unresolved guilt about sexual matters?

6. Do you have fears about sex?

7. How would you rate your sexual performance? Your partner's? How could it be improved?

8. What are different kinds of impotency? What are some causes?

9. Is your body sexually attractive? Is your partner's?

10. What does the Bible prohibit in sex?

11. What is "statistical morality"? How does it differ from Christian ethics?

12. List ways of being creative in the sexual dimension of marriage.

13. How much have you studied the physiology of sex?

5
The Institution and Sanctity of Marriage

If you go to the most skilled carpenter in the world and ask him to build a house, his talent will be worthless unless he knows what a house is. So it is with marriage. It is not easy to build a happy marriage if you have no idea what a marriage is. I used to take for granted that every person in America knows what a marriage is. I don't make that assumption anymore.

In the sixties America witnessed the development of a new "fad"—young people writing their own marriage ceremonies. A race developed to see who could have the most unique or bizarre marriage ceremony. People were married on motorcycles, under the sea wearing aqua lungs, and jumping out of airplanes with parachutes on their backs. This phenomenon was not limited to the secular society but made a visible impact on the Church. Why? What was it that motivated young people to throw out the traditional marriage services in favor of ones created by themselves?

One of the reasons for the movement was a protest against hypocrisy. Young people wanted

their wedding ceremonies to be "meaningful."
They did not want to go through an archaic service
in a perfunctory way, reciting foreign-sounding
phrases that to them represented meaningless
ritual. They felt deeply about marriage and wanted
to know what was going on during the ceremony.
Many of the parents were angered or hurt by the
modernized ceremonies, feeling the loss of a tradition. I had ambivalent feelings when young couples
would ask me to perform wedding ceremonies
which they had written themselves. I was pleased,
of course, that they had invited me to perform
the ceremony. I was also pleased that they wanted
their ceremony to be meaningful to them. I was
alarmed and disappointed, however, when I ex-
amined the ceremonies they wrote. Not one of them
reflected an awareness of the essential ingredients
of a marriage. Their services revealed a very serious ignorance of the institution and sanctity of
marriage.

I find myself being drawn more and more to
the standard, classical form of the wedding ceremony in my church. This is rather odd since I
see this attitude as being foreign to my nature.
I like novelty and experimental things. I like what
is spontaneous and unrehearsed. Perhaps the reason I have grown to love the traditional service
is because I've used it so often. Most laymen do
not get as familiar with the marriage ceremony
as the clergy. Through the repetition and famili-
arity of the service I have come to see that though
it is brief, it is full of meaning. Few words are
wasted; each line deals with a very important ingredient of marriage. As the younger generation
moves away from the service, I feel like Zero
Mostel in *Fiddler on the Roof.*

The play and later screen version of *Fiddler on the Roof* deal poignantly with the loss of tradition. The old Jewish patriarch goes through anguish as one by one his daughters violate the "tradition." In their rebellion the girls ask their father why the tradition has become the tradition. The old man scratches his head and says he doesn't know, but it is the tradition nevertheless. It was good enough for him and for his father and for the father before him. But all of a sudden it is not good enough for the new generation. The tradition is on very precarious ground, threatened by sudden disintegration. The metaphor is clear. The tradition is about as stable as a fiddler on a roof. It is not easy to play a fiddle while perched on a steeply sloped roof. Sooner or later the fiddler will fall. If the tradition does not rest on a solid foundation, then it is doomed to fail.

Is the church's marriage tradition simply an exercise of fiddling? Let's look for a moment at the basic ingredients of the opening statement in the "Order for the Solemnization of Marriage" found in the *Book of Common Worship of the United Presbyterian Church*. It does not differ in substance from those statements used by other Christian communions.

> Dearly beloved, we are assembled here in the presence of God, to join this Man and this Woman in holy marriage; which is instituted by God, regulated by His commandments, blessed by our Lord Jesus Christ, and to be held in honor among all men. Let us therefore reverently remember that God has established and sanctified marriage, for the welfare and happiness of mankind. Our Savior has declared that a man shall leave his

father and mother and cleave unto his wife. By His
apostles, He has instructed those who enter into
this relation to cherish mutual esteem and love;
to bear with each other's infirmities and weak-
nesses; to comfort each other in sickness, trouble, and sorrow; in honesty and industry to provide for each other, and for their household, in
temporal things; to pray for and encourage each
other in the things which pertain to God; and to
live together as the heirs of the grace of life.

In the above-cited liturgy several constituent elements of marriage can be found. In addition to
the instructions regarding cherishing, providing,
etc., we can isolate the following elements that
make up marriage:

1. The ceremony is a public assembly involving a corporate dimension.
2. The ceremony takes place in the presence
of God.
3. Marriage is called holy.
4. Marriage is instituted by God.
5. Marriage is regulated by God's commandments.
6. Marriage is blessed by Jesus Christ.
7. It is stated in the imperative form that marriage is to be held in honor among all men.

Let us examine more closely some of these constituent elements.

Marriage Instituted by God

According to the Christian faith, marriage does
not represent a late development of an advanced
civilization. It doesn't emerge *de nova* on the plain
of history as an arbitrary societal convention.
Rather, the institution of marriage is located in

the divine commandment in creation. As indicated earlier, God sees the creation of woman as fulfilling a decisive need. Perhaps it would be helpful to add to the earlier comments the note that the Genesis account gives special attention to the suitableness of woman to fulfill man. We read:

> And out of the ground the Lord God formed every beast of the field and every bird of the sky, and brought them to the man to see what he would call them; and whatever the man called a living creature, that was its name. And the man gave names to all the cattle, and to all the birds of the sky, and to every beast of the field, but for Adam there was not found a helper suitable for him. (Gen. 2:19-20)

Prior to the creation of woman, man was alone. That loneliness received the malediction of God. Then God created the plants and the animals. Now man was no longer utterly alone. But he did not have a suitable partner. So God created woman to fulfill humanity. Martin Luther saw a relationship between woman's sexual capacity and her suitability. In other forms of life we often see a discrepancy between the male and female capacity for sexual involvement For example, among dogs the male is ready and able to have sexual relations anytime during the year. But the female is interested only when she is in heat, normally about twice a year. That can create a lot of frustration for Fido. He may complain to his Creator about giving him a less than suitable partner. Man can register no such complaint. Luther commented, "Isn't it nice that God provided such a suitable mate?" (At another time and in another mood Luther also commented, "If God wanted me to have a meek woman, He would have to hew one out of stone.'')

In understanding the divine institution of marriage, it is important to notice that marriage was not merely for Jews or for Christians. Marriage is instituted in the Covenant of Creation. That means it was instituted for man as man, not for man as Jew or as Christian. All men come under the authority of this institution. (That is why the marriage service calls attention to the fact that marriage is to be held in honor among all men.) Men may refuse to acknowledge God's authority over marriage or refuse to even acknowledge His existence. But that does not change the fact that they are held accountable by God for the honoring of the divine institution of marriage. Men may deny their relationship to God, but they have that relationship nevertheless.

That marriage is blessed by Christ is seen clearly in the New Testament teaching about it. His presence and participation at the wedding feast of Cana is further evidence of that blessing. The supreme evidence of His blessing, however, is found in His consideration of the Church as His bride.

Regulated by His Commandments

The idea of divine institution carries with it the implication of God's sovereign authority to regulate what He institutes. Again the regulations listed in Scripture are not many in number but they are significant. For example, marriage is restricted to one man and one woman. Homosexual marriage is forbidden explicitly, and polygamy

116

is forbidden implicitly. It is sometimes difficult
to see the crucial character of monogamy since
several outstanding characters of the Old Testament openly practice polygamy. Jacob, David,
Solomon, etc., all had more than one wife. But
the situation in creation does not reflect polygamy.
God created one wife for Adam, not two. He said
that the "two" should become one flesh, not
"three." More to the point is a very important
aspect of the early chapters of Genesis that is
often overlooked in the debate over polygamy ver-
sus monogamy. In chapters 4 and 5 of Genesis
we have the "begatitudes." That is, we find the
geneological tables of the descendants of Adam.
The list is very significant as two separate lines
are traced. The first is the line of the descendants
of Cain, and the second is the line of the descendants of Seth, the third son of Adam and Eve.
Now it is through the line of Seth that the patriar-
chal blessing comes. It is this line that produces
a gallery of righteous people. This line includes
Enoch who "walked with God," and Methuselah
and, most importantly, Noah. The line of Cain,
however, traces the history of radical degeneration
and corruption that follows closely upon the murder
of Abel. The line of Cain represents a kind of
"Rogue's Gallery" of antiquity. One of the worst
rogues mentioned in the list is Lamech who is
noted for his love of violence. Lamech is also mentioned as the first to practice polygamy. Most commentators find in the brief description of the text
a strongly implicit judgment on polygamy. That
God exercised forbearance with David, Jacob,
etc., does not mean that He sanctioned their polygamy. Nowhere does God give His blessing to a
plural marriage.

In setting forth the principles of marriage, the Scriptures give us clear teaching with respect to the regulation of divorce. That teaching is so important that we will deal with it later in a separate chapter.

Another regulatory principle that is found both in the Old Covenant and the New Covenant is the principle forbidding the marriage of a believer to an unbeliever. Paul, indeed, gives certain instructions to those who are involved in a mixed marriage, but that presupposes a situation that develops when two unbelievers marry and then one of them becomes a believer. This regulation has provoked much debate and consternation among church members. One of the most difficult tasks a clergyman has is to enforce this regulation and try to keep peace in the church at the same time.

Imagine what happens when Suzy, filled with radiant joy and eager expectations, comes to see the pastor and asks him to perform her wedding to John. The pastor nervously asks John if he is a Christian. John candidly replies that he is not but that he has no objections about his wife's "religion." Then the pastor painfully explains to the young couple that according to his own conscience, he is unable to perform the ceremony. All the while the pastor knows that his words are very likely to be taken by the couple as an expression of narrow-minded prejudice. He also knows that the pastor down the street will willingly perform the ceremony and add further credence to the idea that the first pastor was a bigot. What's worse is that the pastor also is aware that Suzy's father is an elder in the church and will most likely call that evening and say, "What do you mean, you won't marry our daughter? Isn't she good enough to be married in this church? What do we pay your salary for anyway? My daughter was baptized in this church, and confirmed in this church and, by thunder, she is going to be married in this church!" So the pastor either relents to keep the corporate peace or he goes into hiding to keep his own peace.

After counseling couples ravaged by the results of mixed marriages, I've come to a greater respect for the wisdom of God. Where religious faith doesn't mean much to either partner the problems over religion are usually not great—this marriage is "mixed" on paper, not in reality. Where a vital faith is present in one partner, however, very serious problems of conflict emerge. It is particularly difficult when it is the woman who is the Christian. If she takes seriously the mandate to be submissive to her husband, she finds herself confronted with the unenviable task of trying to serve two masters. We find a serious conflict of values, of approaches to dealing with children, and a multitude of other problems. When a man tries to live as a Christian and his wife is an unbeliever, he finds that when he needs the support of his helpmate, she isn't there.

Sometimes the situations that develop in mixed marriages are humorous. On one occasion I listened to a man give a public address about the rigors of living with a Christian wife. Though he was not a Christian, his wife was very zealous. She was deeply involved in the work of the church and was involved with a lay-evangelism team. In his speech he commented, "My wife never tells me anything. When I ask her about something, she doesn't just simply tell me but she says, 'Let me share it with you.' I feel like I'm about to get a stock dividend with all this 'sharing.' "

For the Welfare and Happiness of Man

One of the most difficult principles for mankind to accept is the principle that God's regulations are designed for our happiness. In the "Land of the Free" we say that rules are made to be broken. We seem to have a built-in antipathy to restrictions. The word "forbidden" seems to ring a bell of defiance within us. Often we assume that laws will inevitably restrict our happiness. I had to struggle with this early in my exposure to the Christian faith. As a boy I was required to attend communicants' class at church. In the class we had to memorize the Westminster Shorter Catechism. I didn't do well in the class, but I do remember the first question. It reads, "What is man's chief end?" It wasn't the question that bothered me but the answer that gave me fits. "Man's chief end is to glorify God and enjoy Him forever." This sounded to me like a contradiction in terms. I knew enough to figure out that to glorify God meant to keep His commandments. But I didn't see how that could produce joy. I was in the "what I like is either immoral, illegal, or fattening" syndrome. It wasn't until much later in life that I discovered the Law of God was not designed by a capricious tyrant in order to keep His people miserable. I learned that He was the God of Moses who heard the groans of His people and had led them out of chains, not into them. I discovered the He was the one who created male-

ness and femaleness and provided marriage for
human well-being.

What human situation is more full of complexities than marriage? Here every conceivable nu-
ance of human behavior is brought into play. To
know your way around the labyrinth of marriage
requires more wisdom than Solomon had. Even
Howard Cosell would grope for words trying to
call the "blow by blow" of the marriage spat.
Is there any place in our lives where we need
transcendent wisdom more desperately than in
marriage? And that is precisely what is provided
for us in the regulations of God.

At this point I would like to make a rather
bold assertion. In every single marriage that ends
in disaster some *stupid* decisions were made with
respect to God's regulations. If God's regulations
were followed scrupulously, there would be not
only no divorces, there would be no unhappy marriages. To violate the regulations of God is not
only an exercise in disobedience but an exercise
in foolishness as well. If you want a happy marriage, the most intelligent thing you can do is to
submit to God's regulations. They are designed
to promote and protect your full happiness. God
carefully planned them. But before the regulations
of God can work for our happiness, we have to
know what they are. Again, study is required that
we may not only *know* the wisdom of God but
that we *master* it. (In my college classes the difference between an A and a B was the difference
between knowledge and mastery of the material.)
Who wants to be satisfied with anything less than
an A marriage?

Confidence in the wisdom of God is closely re-

lated to our obedience to Him. The great delusion
is contained in the thought, "If I keep His commandments I will not be happy." Herein is the
fundamental human delusion. There may of course
be *pleasure* in disobedience but there can never
be *happiness*. And happiness in the biblical sense
is more than a warm puppy. When I experience
a conflict of interests or a conflict of desires between what I want and what God requires, then
I know the moral crisis of sin. When I choose my
own desire and insult the integrity of God's wisdom, I at the same time reveal myself to be a
fool.

Marriage as a Covenant

We Presbyterians have a tendency to think
about everything in terms of covenant. Perhaps
it is because so much of human life is arranged
in the structure of a covenant. Not only is the
covenant principle central to the Bible, but it is
a basic ingredient of the American way of life.
Simply stated, a covenant is an agreement between
two or more parties and is binding upon the persons
involved.

We see this worked out at every level of human
existence. For example, at the economic-social
level the covenant form is seen daily. I don't merely show up for work at Procter and Gamble or
United States Steel, sit down at a desk, put in
a few hours and go to the office to collect my
wages. When I am employed I enter into a contract
or covenant relation with my employer. There are
specific terms and obligations which are binding
upon both parties. I am required to perform certain

duties, put in so many hours of labor, etc., and the employer agrees to provide certain benefits, including wages, etc. The covenant basis of an industrial contract came home to me rudely only last night. After a hard day's work (the work involved being on a diet), I sat down to a succulent steak dinner. After only three bites of the tasty meat the telephone rang. It was a friend calling to tell me that the local gas station had just reopened. I dropped my fork, ran to the closet for my coat and hastened to the gas station where I waited in line for half an hour to get my tank filled. I came home to a cold dinner, but I wore a satisfied smile. I was greatly relieved to get that gas. At this point in the truckers' strike it is more important to fill my car than my stomach. With fuel shortage, violence on the highways, and waiting lines in the supermarkets, we are being made keenly aware of industrial contracts and their bearing on our lives. (One news commentator said recently, "With all these strikes, America is beginning to look more like a bowling alley than a nation.")

Perhaps in the political area of our lives we feel the crunch of the covenant principle even more keenly. There have been many forms of government in world history and a wide variety of political theories in competition to one another. We have seen monarchy, oligarchy, de:aocracy, plutocracy, autocracy, and a host of others. The form of government by which our nation was founded was a form of the Social Contract theory, developed in England by the famous philosopher John Locke. It was transplanted and revised for this country largely through the genius of Thomas Jefferson.

In our form of the Social Contract, the government rules within the context of a covenant relation with the people. That our nation opted for a covenant form in its government when it declared its independence is not strange. The very first form of government implemented in our land over 150 years before the constitution was framed was the Mayflower Compact. In the Mayflower Compact the covenant principle was heavily stressed.

The covenant of our government is renewed at every inauguration ceremony and installation of political officials. The rulers are required to swear an oath that they will uphold the constitution of the United States and work to promote the well-being of the nation. Their vows are to be enforced by the judicial branch of the government. At the same time the people are called to pledge their allegiance to their government. They must pay their taxes, serve in the army, etc. If the pledge is violated, penalties are evoked. We have lived through a traumatic period in our nation's history; we have witnessed the violation of covenant trust in the highest offices of government. The office of the President himself has been rocked with the scandal of Watergate.

At no level of our lives, however, does the covenant form touch us more deeply than at the level of marriage. It is at this point that we see an almost unbelievable ignorance of covenant. It is common-place in our day to hear students ask, "Why should we get married? How can a few words and a ceremony suddenly make it legal? Why can't two people just agree between themselves to live together and let that be that?" These people say the marriage ceremony is a farce and a charade. They can't see any point in it. This, of course, betrays a profound ignorance of covenant in general and marriage in particular.

At the heart of the institution of marriage is the reality of commitment. In biblical categories, this commitment is not one that takes place privately in a corner. It is a public matter. Hence the very beginning of the marriage ceremony calls attention to the fact that the "dearly beloved" are gathered in an assembly before witnesses. The marriage ceremony is a corporate affair. The Bible has low regard for private covenants witnessed by no one. A frequently misunderstood verse of the Bible is the one that contains the famous "Mizpah Benediction." The benediction states, "May the Lord watch between me and thee, while we are absent, one from another." It sounds like very nice and friendly words. They are used to dismiss countless Sunday school and youth group meetings. But how were the words originally used? Let's look at the context.

> So Jacob took a stone, and set it up as a pillar. And Jacob said to his kinsmen, "Gather stones," And they took stones, and made a heap; and they ate there by the heap. . . . Laban said, "This heap is a witness between you and me today." Therefore he named it Galeed, and the pillar Mizpah, for he said, "The Lord watch between you and me, when we are absent one from the other. If you ill-treat my daughters, or if you take wives besides my daughters, although no man is with us, remember, God is witness between you and me." (Gen. 31:45-50, RSV)

Now, what is going on here between Jacob and Laban? This is not a covenant between friends.

There was no love lost between Jacob and Laban. They didn't have a great deal of trust for one another. Jacob was famous for his chicanery, and Laban was not exactly a pillar of trustworthiness. This was a covenant between thieves who didn't trust each other as far as they could throw an elephant. Laban was not saying to Jacob, "God be with you and protect you till we meet again." Laban was not interested in invoking God to protect Jacob; he wanted God to protect Laban. He was saying to Jacob, "I hope God watches you like a hawk so you won't pull any more fast ones on me." They wanted witnesses to their "covenant" so badly that they set up rocks because there weren't any people around without vested interests.

Why is it so important for us to have witnesses to our covenants or to sign legal documents when we make them? There are several reasons for this practice—not the least is the fact that our lives often depend on the trustworthiness of commitments. Another reason is that human history has demonstrated, if nothing else, that people do not always keep their promises. This is seen in the Bible as the basic qualitative difference between God and man. God is tethered by chains to His own truthfulness. Yet He declares that "all men are liars." The devil is called the father of lies. God is a covenant-keeper, while man is a covenant-breaker. To protect man from his own fallen humanity, God requires witnesses and sanctions to covenants. Even God himself makes a ceremony when He enters a covenant with Abraham (see Gen. 15). The New Testament tells us that because He can swear by no higher than himself, God swears by himself when He makes a covenant with us. He pledges His own self-destruction if He fails to keep His word. How much does a covenant cost that is made in the back seat of a car between two lovers? The issue in a marriage ceremony is focused on one basic question, "Can I trust your word?"

The marriage estate is the most vulnerable state of human existence. Here is where we have the most to lose. Here is where we are absolutely open and vulnerable. Here commitment means everything. When people are married in a public ceremony, involving witnesses and the signing of paper, and if they later desire to repudiate that commitment, they cannot simply say to their partner, "It's your word against mine." When two people stand up in a church and exchange vows, it is a significant occasion. The vows are made in public rather than in private. They are made in the presence of every authority that means anything to the people involved. They state their vows in front of each other, in front of their parents, their relatives, their friends, the ecclesiastical authorities, and in front of the authority of the state. And all of this is done "in the presence of God." That is a public commitment. If the couple do not take their vows seriously, perhaps their family or friends or church will. If none of those do, the state will take it somewhat seriously (though certainly not as seriously as it ought to); a divorce will cost something. One thing is certain, God will take those vows very seriously.

The idea of rugged individualism has so permeated our thinking that frequently people think that everything they do is their own business and nobody else's. The philosophy is "everyone do his own thing." I once had an experience with a college student who came to see me because he was having trouble getting along with his mother. He told me that he was an atheist and his mother was a very zealous Christian. He said he was sick of his mother "trying to ram religion down my throat." In the course of the conversation, the boy revealed to me that he thought there were no absolute values or rules for living. He said that everyone ought to have the right to do his own thing. His ethics were his own affair and his mother didn't have a right to disapprove. He insisted that each person should be able to do as he pleased. I asked him, "Do you really believe that?" He emphatically stated that he did. So I asked him the obvious question, "Then why do you object when your mother tries to cram religion down your throat? Doesn't she also have the right to do as she pleases? Maybe her 'thing' is cramming religion down people's throats." His eyes widened and you could see the little lightbulb going on over his head as he said, "I never thought of that!"

When people start doing their own thing with no consideration for anyone else, other people will get hurt. Again I saw the corporate dimension of marriage very vividly in a counseling case involving an affair. I talked with the offending husband and his other woman. They told me that what they were doing was their own business and nobody else's. I disagreed. In the course of that particular case, I was involved with counseling exactly 28 people. I counted them. I had to deal with the two already mentioned and the injured wife, but it didn't stop there. I became involved with the

parents of all three of them as well as grand-
parents, children, and other relatives. Close
friends of all three came to me for help in dealing
with the situation. A lot of people suffered from
just two people's "own business." When violence
was threatened I had to provide shelter for one
of the persons involved. When I had to go out of
town I had to bring in representatives of the law
to protect my own family during my absence. The
affair was not a private thing. Marriage involves
many more people than simply the husband and
the wife. Thus the marriage is contracted not only
in the presence of God (whose presence extends,
by the way, to the office of the Justice of the Peace
as well as to the church building) but in the presence of human witnesses who are called to testify
or bear witness to the truth.

All of our statements come under the scrutiny
of God. We are warned in the New Testament
that every idle word we speak will be brought
to the judgment. If God takes our idle words seriously, how much more seriously does He take those
words spoken with forethought? And if He takes
our normal statements seriously, how much more
seriously does He take our promises, especially
when those promises are raised to the level of
the formal vow? All of our vows and oaths come
under the authority of God. We seem to have a
particular problem realizing that in the United
States. In Europe we have the sad reputation of
not keeping our promises. After meeting a Dutch
fellow one evening in Amsterdam and enjoying
casual conversation with him, I ended the conversation by saying, "We'll have to have you over
to our apartment sometime for dinner." My face

turned red as he immediately took out his pen and his pocket calendar and said, "When?" I realized how often we make statements like that which we don't mean at all. (I had no intention of really inviting that man to my home for dinner. I must confess, however, that I'm glad I did because out of that dinner-meeting grew a warm and lasting relationship.)

The idea of a "ceremony" for marriage is not an American invention. All over the world, even in the most remote primitive tribes, people have ceremonies for marriage. People dance, dress in their finest garments, prepare their best foods, and go through all kinds of rituals. Why? Perhaps because it is deeply rooted in the collective consciousness of mankind that marriage is a very special thing and that the commitment involved is not a casual one. The ceremony dimension of marriage is in our human bloodstream, and those who marry without it are missing something special.

The Marriage Vows

In order to gain a better understanding of the content and meaning of the marriage vows, let us again look briefly at the vows contained in the United Presbyterian Book of Common Worship. Most marriage vows correspond to these.

> I, ———, take thee, ———; To be my wedded wife (or husband); And I do promise and covenant; Before God and these witnesses; To be thy loving and faithful husband; In plenty and in want; In joy and in sorrow; In sickness and in health; As long as we both shall live.

What is promised in these vows? What kind

of a commitment is being made here? Basically two things are promised in the vows: *love* and *fidelity*. We have already discussed at length what it means to be loving. What is meant by fidelity? It means maintaining the honor of the marriage by keeping the terms of the covenant. This is why marital infidelity is so serious. It cuts at the heart of the marriage contract. It violates the deepest part of the commitment.

Under what circumstances are the vows to be maintained? The first vow mentioned is in plenty or in want. The vows are to remain intact regardless of the financial circumstances of the marriage. The commitment is not to depend on money. If poverty comes the spouse does not have the right to seek another partner who can provide a better financial situation or offer more luxury. Nor can the partner dissolve the covenant when great riches suddenly come, seeking another partner more accustomed to a higher standard of living.

The second vow involves joy and sorrow. Being married to a person who does not bring the level of joy desired is not an excuse to leave the marriage. If tragedy strikes the home, bringing grief, there is still no reason to walk out.

The third circumstance that is mentioned is that of health. When the fine physical specimen you marry is ravaged by age or disease, these are not grounds for breaking your promise. When your wife becomes 40 years old, you cannot trade her in for two 20-year-olds.

These vows do not specifically state every possible circumstance that might arise and affect the marriage. The wedding ceremony would last for hours if every eventuality were dealt with explicitly. But the spirit of the vows contains implicitly all of these possible circumstances. What the vows are expressing is a promise of love and fidelity in all kinds of circumstances.

The vows involve a lot more than providing only a present declaration of love. A person must not enter marriage saying, "I love you today, but I might not tomorrow," nor, "I promise to love you if everything goes well." The vows are not merely a declaration of present love and fidelity but a declaration and commitment to *future* love and fidelity. Many of you who are reading this book took those vows a long time ago; what was future then is present right now.

And what is the duration of the obligation to keep the vow? Is there an annual review clause in the marriage? Can one commit himself for five or ten years? Not by these vows. The vow here is "as long as we both shall live." The commitment of marriage is a commitment for life.

In addition to the marriage vows there is the pledge of troth (loyalty). I will reproduce it here without comment:

> ————, wilt thou have this man (or woman) to be thy husband, and wilt thou pledge thy troth to him, in all love and honor, in all duty and service, in all faith and tenderness, to live with him, and cherish him, according to the ordinance of God, in the holy bond of marriage?

One thing is clear in the vows and the pledge of troth: marriage is not a casual alliance or a temporary experiment. It is a bond, a holy bond, permanently cemented by a commitment. When young people ask me, "How do I know when I am deeply enough in love to get married?" I always provide a standard or "pat" answer. The answer is pat because it is so true, "When you love him enough to publicly commit yourself to that person for the rest of your life." Such a commitment involves a tremendous amount of risk. But that is the kind of commitment necessary to make us "naked and unashamed."

Questions for Discussion

1. Why do people want to write their own wedding ceremonies?

2. If you wrote your own wedding ceremony, what would you include in it?

3. Why did God institute marriage?

4. Are God's laws foolish and oppressive?

5. Why does the Church recognize civil marriages?

6. What is a covenant? How many covenant relationships are you in?

7. Why should covenants have witnesses?

8. Why does God prohibit "mixed marriages"?

9. What is the difference between pleasure and happiness?

10. What is a vow? What is the meaning of marriage vows? How long are the vows in effect?

6
What About Divorce?

If we recognize the fact that marriage is regulated by God's commandments, we are forced to face the implications of those regulations for divorce. Divorce is messy business and needs to be approached with great care and soberness. The purpose of this chapter is to examine several facets of the divorce question. We will look briefly at the current divorce climate of our culture, then examine closely the biblical teaching on the matter, with special attention to Jesus' teaching on the subject. Then we will look at some of the practical dynamics of divorce-counseling. Since the divorce question is one that is frequently charged with great emotion, it would be advisable to consider the chapter as a whole. The chapter comes at this point in the book in the hope that the reader will have been prepared for it by the preceding chapters.

The Divorce Crisis in America

Whenever a group of gray-heads get together and wring their hands and cluck their tongues over

the decadence and corruption of the new generation, lament the fact that the younger generation
is "going to the dogs," and wax eloquent about
the "good old days," it is inevitable that their
lament is met by the knowing smiles of those enlightened by history. Sooner or later someone will
trap the old-timers by reading a detailed description of youthful degeneration into bad manners,
disrespect for parents, tradition, etc., and then
stun the listeners by announcing that the description was written by Solon, Pericles, Socrates
or some other sage of antiquity. The point of such
a quotation, of course, is to demonstrate that as
long as there have been human generations, there
have been those who thought the new generation
was going to the dogs and was taking everyone
to the kennels with them. It is a common oc-
currence for older generations to view the younger
generations with a jaundiced eye. Nostalgia for
the old days and contempt for the modern ones
is based more often on impressions than on facts.

However things may tend to remain the same,
there are some areas of the corporate life of a
society that can be measured other than by nos-
talgic impressions. One of those areas is the institution of marriage. In our society marriages and
divorces are matters of legal records and can be
measured statistically.

Today our prophets of doom are found not so
much in the pulpits of our churches as in the bur-
eaus of our secular institutions. In 1948 the famous
Harvard sociologist Pitirim A. Sorokin lamented
the measurable increase in violence and divorce
in American society as manifestations of inevitable
social disintegration. He said at the time:

An illiterate society can survive, but a thoroughly anti-social society cannot. Until recently the family was the principal school of socialization for the new-born human animals, rendering them fit for social life. At present this vital mission is performed less and less by the family.

Sorokin's concern was triggered by what he regarded as an alarming change in the divorce rate in America. He expressed shock and dismay that the divorce rate in America had "risen sharply" from 1 in 10 in 1910 to 1 in 4 in 1948. Thus, in the short span of 38 years, the incidence of divorce in America rose from 10 percent to 25 percent, or an increase of 150 percent.

It would be nice to report that Sorokin's alarm was rashly voiced and that he underestimated American society's ability to correct the disintegrating situation. It would be nice to say that the marriage situation has stabilized and that the fiber of the American family has been solidified. Such a report, however, would be whistling in the dark. A more accurate picture reveals that the divorce rate has not stabilized but accelerated. In 1970 the rate had risen to 40 percent or 2 out of 5 marriages ending in divorce. In 1970 the statistics reached 50 percent of all teenage marriages and 50 percent of marriages in California. By 1973, the overall divorce rate rose to between 45 and 50 percent. Thus, in the space of 63 years since 1910 the divorce rate has risen from 1 in 10 to 5 in 10—an increase of 400 percent.

What about the future? It doesn't require a genius or an expert statistician to chart the current trend. Our secular institutions have responded to the rapid proliferation of divorces not by moving to make a divorce more difficult to obtain but by facilitating the process. The current trend is toward making divorce easier via no-fault divorce legislation and/or the broadening of the grounds for divorce. Such action cannot possibly retard the growth rate of divorce but will inevitably increase it. What will be the future of a society where more than half of the family units will be broken by divorce? If there ever was a time for a citizen to jump up and down screaming "Foul!" it's now. We as a nation have already gone far beyond the point of diminishing returns. It is no small matter that the family unit is imperiled. Divorce is a very serious business.

The Teaching of Jesus on Divorce

When the Christian faces the issue of divorce, he must come to grips with the teaching of Jesus on the subject. Here is a vital test of a person's submission to the authority of Christ. At this point the question of the lordship of Christ moves out of the realm of the abstract and into the bloodstream of daily life. The question of marriage and divorce is a question Jesus spoke to directly. Let's examine Matthew's account of the Pharisee's interrogation of Jesus on the issue.

> And Pharisees came up to him, and tested him by asking, "Is it lawful for a man to divorce his wife for any cause at all?" And he answered and said, "Have you not read, that he who created them from the beginning made them male and female, and said, 'for this cause a man shall leave his father and mother, and shall cleave to his wife; and the two shall become one

flesh'? Consequently they are no more two, but one flesh. What therefore God has joined together, let no man separate." They said to him, "Why then did Moses command to give her a certificate and divorce her?" He said to them, "Because of your hardness of heart, Moses permitted you to divorce your wives; but from the beginning it has not been this way. And I say to you, whoever divorces his wife, except for immorality, and marries another commits adultery."

The disciples said to him, "If the relationship of the man with his wife is like this, it is better not to marry." (Matt. 19:3-10)

Having glanced at the account of the conversation with the Pharisees in its entirety, let's now look more closely at the details of the discussion. The discourse is introduced by the editorial comment, "The Pharisees come to him, *testing* him. . . ." What was the nature of the test? To answer that question requires some research and reconstruction of the circumstances surrounding the debate.

The reason for the "testing" can be found in the hostility the Pharisees clearly manifested toward Jesus. If they could trap Him in a theological error, they could discredit His teachings. If they could get Jesus to side with one of the other Rabbinic schools which were hotly divided on the issue of divorce, they could alienate Him from at least one faction. If they could get Jesus to contradict Moses, they could charge Him with undermining the Law of God. Finally, it is important to keep in mind that the debate takes place in the territory where Herod Antipas was the ruling tetrarch. It was Herod Antipas who had John the Baptist imprisoned and subsequently killed because he said to Herod, "It is not lawful for you to have your brother's wife" (Mark 6:18).

The nature of the "test" becomes more clear when we see the precise question the Pharisees put to Jesus: "Is it lawful for a man to divorce his wife for any cause at all?" This question is precisely the debate between the two leading Rabbinic schools of Jesus' day. It involves the interpretation of the Old Testament law. It is a legal question. Notice the question is not, "Is it lawful for a man to divorce his wife?", but the issue is, "Is it lawful to divorce *for any cause at all.*" Both Rabbinic schools agreed that divorce was lawful, but what are the *grounds* of a lawful divorce?

The rabbis differed sharply on the grounds. The two schools of thought were the schools of Shammai and Hillel. Broadly speaking, the Hillel school was liberal and the Shammai school conservative. They disputed with each other over the interpretation of Deut. 24:1.

> When a man takes a wife and marries her, and it happens that she finds no favor in his eyes because he has found some indecency in her, and he writes her a certificate of divorce and puts it in her hand and sends her out from his house. . . .

The argument focused on the interpretation of the words "some indecency." The word "indecency" is somewhat ambiguous, and thus the argument raged over what kind of an indecency was legal grounds for divorce.

The Shammai school took a very narrow view of the "indecency" mentioned. They interpreted "indecency" as referring to some grossly shameful act such as sexual infidelity. On the other hand, the Hillel school took a broad and lax view of the matter, granting divorce for almost anything. Hillel permitted divorce if the wife burned the food she was cooking or broke one of her husband's favorite dishes. Rabbi Akiba permitted divorce if the husband discovered a more attractive woman. It seems evident that popular Jewish opinion followed the Hillel school in its liberal view. The Jewish historian Josephus indicated that divorce could be granted "for any cause whatsoever."

Thus the question of the rabbis is put to Jesus. If He sides with Hillel, He can be charged with moral laxity by the conservatives. If He sides with Shammai, He alienates the Hillel school and popular opinion and risks the wrath of Herod Antipas.

How does Jesus answer the question? At first glance it may appear that He was cleverly evasive. He does not immediately address himself to the interpretation of Deuteronomy 24. Instead He cites the creation passage about the original institution of marriage, ending His response with the quotation, "What therefore God has joined together, let no man separate." He prefaces His citation with the question, "Have you not read, that he who created them . . .?" There was not much flattery in the question. Imagine Jesus asking these teachers if they had read the first few chapters of the book they were supposed to be teaching about; this was equivalent to Jesus' asking, "Do you fellows ever read the Bible?" The force of the citation, however, goes beyond this not-so-subtle rebuke and forces the Pharisees to consider the issue in the total biblical context. They had been isolating the Mosaic law out of the broader framework of God's original intent with the institution of marriage. In effect, Jesus is saying, "If there is ambiguity in the Law of Moses, let the implications you draw be governed by what God spoke clearly in creation."

The Pharisees don't beat around the bush any further and immediately pursue the issue of the Law of Moses: "Why then did Moses command to give her a certificate and divorce her?" The point of the question is obvious. If God never intended divorce, why did He authorize Moses to "command" divorce? Jesus' answer is direct. "Because of your hardness of heart Moses permitted you to divorce your wives; but from the beginning it has not been this way." Notice the change in words. The Pharisees talk about Moses *commanding* divorce; Jesus talks about Moses *permitting* divorce. A command leaves no option— it must be carried out. Permission is less forceful, giving the party an option. Jesus interprets the Mosaic law as *permission* for divorce granted because of the *hardness* of the heart. This reflects an act of condescension to accommodate the influence of sin upon the marriage estate. But He repeats His point that in creation there was no provision for divorce.

Finally Jesus deals directly with the issue by rendering His verdict. "And I say to you, Whoever divorces his wife, except for immorality, and marries another commits adultery." Here the ambiguity of the "indecency" is cleared up. The grounds that Jesus provides for divorce are immorality. The immorality in view is specifically sexual immorality or fornication as the Greek *porneia* is used. Here Jesus clearly repudiates the liberal view of divorce championed by the Hillel school

We are forced to draw the conclusion from this

text that Jesus took a very dim view of divorce. He allows it (in a spirit of guarded reluctancy) but only in the case of fornication or adultery (sexual immorality). Even in the case of permissible grounds, the higher calling is to preserve the original intent of the marriage institution, i.e., the indissolubility of marriage. That Jesus took a "hard stance" on this point is reflected clearly in the disciples' reaction: "If the relationship of the man with his wife is like this, it is better not to marry." Notice this isn't the stunned response of the Pharisees, but of Jesus' own disciples. They would have hardly reacted this way if Jesus had given a liberal view of divorce.

Additional information on the divorce issue is provided us by the Apostle Paul in his first letter to the Corinthians. Paul gives instructions to the church, saying:

> But to the married I give instructions, not I, but the Lord, that the wife should not leave her husband (but is she does leave, let her remain unmarried, or else be reconciled to her husband), and that the husband should not send his wife away. But to the rest I say, not the Lord, that if any brother has a wife who is an unbeliever, and she consents to live with him, let him not send her away. And a woman who has an unbelieving husband he consents to live with her, let her not send her husband away . . . Yet if the unbelieving one leaves, let him leave; the brother or the sister is not under bondage in such cases, but God has called us to peace. (I Cor. 7:10-13, 15)

Here Paul gives instructions that apply to the situation of a mixed marriage. Note that Paul does not sanction the entrance into marriage with an unbeliever but is dealing with a situation in an existing marriage. What happens when two unbelievers are married and one of them becomes a Christian and the other wants to separate? Paul's instructions are clear in at least some points. The believer is not to initiate proceedings for separation or desertion from the unbeliever. The believer is free, however, if the unbeliever initiates the separation. There is a question here about the meaning of separation. Some have argued that in the desertion of the unbeliever, the believer is not obliged to seek reconciliation but is free to exist in a state of separation but not divorce (unless the unbeliever remarries). Others have maintained that Paul is providing not only a basis for legal separation but legitimate divorce, namely desertion of the nonbeliever. Thus for Christians there are two possible grounds for divorce: (1) sexual immorality, (2) desertion of the unbeliever.

Without delving into the technicalities that are involved in Paul's meaning of "separation," we can at least reach some preliminary conclusions:

1. No more than two grounds are recognized by Scripture as grounds for divorce.

2. A Christian is permitted to *initiate* divorce proceedings only in the case of sexual immorality.

3. A Christian is free, *at least* to be separated if deserted by a nonbeliever.

4. The original intent and goal of marriage is no divorce.

If the above conclusions are correct, what does this mean for our culture? In the first place it means that there are many Hillels loose in the land. It means that the civil courts are disrupting the commandments of God in granting illicit divorces. It means that in many cases the institutional church has sanctioned divorce on grounds that are in clear opposition to the teaching of Christ. It means that clergymen and counselors through the land are recommending divorce where Christ has prohibited it. It means that not only is the sanctity of marriage corrupted by both state and church, but the authority of Christ is flagrantly disobeyed in both spheres over which He is King. The word for such disobedience is *treason*.

The Dynamics of Divorce Counseling

How does one apply the biblical ethic of marriage and divorce to real life situations involving real persons with crushing problems? How can the counselor maintain his commitment to the authority of Christ without compromise in the face of overwhelming cultural pressure to conform to the lax standards of the day? How can a pastor manifest compassion in the face of a marriage characterized by misery without recommending divorce? These are only a few of the sticky questions a Christian pastor or counselor must deal with in actual practice. To sing the Lord's song in an alien land is as difficult for a Christian in America as it ever was for a Jew in Babylon.

To begin with, the pastor or counselor must have confidence in several things: (1) The reality of God's sovereign authority in regulating marriage. (2) The reality of God's wisdom in that regulation. (3) The reality of God's design in regulating for the purpose of the welfare and happiness of man. If we are convinced that God's regulations are established for our happiness and welfare, we can never fall into the trap of thinking that disobedience will bring happiness or well-being. Disobedience can bring pleasure or quick relief from pain (which is why it is so often attractive) but it cannot bring happiness.

In addition to the confidence in the wisdom, authority and benevolence of God, the counselor must have genuine love and compassion. He must love the persons enough to counsel them against their desires. He must have enough compassion to lead them into pain if it is necessary for healing, risking their personal danger or alienation to protect them from making serious mistakes. He must be compassionate enough to risk being accused of not being compassionate enough. (Is there any accusation to which the Christian is more vulnerable than the charge that he is not loving?)

I am convinced not only by theory but by considerable practice that if the above ingredients are present in counseling, an astonishing amount of healing of broken marriages can be seen.

When a couple comes to the pastor for marriage/divorce counseling, the marriage is usually already in serious trouble. To simplify matters the couple usually has about three concrete options from which to choose: (1) They can choose to maintain the status quo. (2) They can seek a divorce. (3) They can try to establish a redeemed marriage. These are the basic options: status quo, divorce, or redeemed marriage.

I find the options are usually faced like this. The status quo is utterly intolerable and is desired by no one, so is not really a live option. Divorce is considered painful and messy, but it at least offers relief from the intolerable situation of the status quo and offers the hope of a new start and a new life. The idea of a redeemed marriage is viewed as a utopian dream which in light of the status quo is deemed virtually impossible. Too many wounds would have to be healed, too many changes would have to take place, etc.

Thus when a couple comes with serious marriage problems, practically speaking they see only two real options, status quo or divorce. If the status quo is indeed intolerable, the option of divorce becomes highly desirable. If these are the only options, most people will choose divorce.

But what happens if the option of divorce is removed? If it is seen as being firmly prohibited, the couple is left with two alternatives—status quo or a redeemed marriage. When these alternatives are in view it is nothing less than amazing to see the sudden willingness of one or both parties to undergo the necessary changes and discipline for a redeemed marriage, even if those changes are severely painful. The situation is somewhat comparable to people faced with chronic illness and pain who are willing to undergo radical surgery or painful therapy in order to alleviate their misery. If a toothache is bad enough, most people are willing to face the dentist's drill. But if there is some other less painful procedure that offers relief from the ache, the average American will try it. We are a nation of unrefined hedonists, always seeking the less painful route.

Marriages can't be healed or redeemed overnight. There is no therapeutic panacea that can transform an intolerable marriage situation into an idyllic dream. But the *direction* of the marriage can change overnight. The pattern of destruction can change into a pattern of construction in a very short time. For this pattern to change a new commitment must be made. If the two options are status quo or redemption, that commitment is not difficult to make. But if the options include divorce, commitment is extremely difficult. If the option of divorce is not chosen but remains a serious consideration, a person is usually paralyzed and cannot make the kind of commitment necessary to change the direction of the marriage. This situation tends to make a person "halt between two opinions," waiting for the partner to initiate the decision or for "something to happen" that will push the partner one way or the other.

The power necessary to rebuild a broken marriage may be the moral power of duty. It is clear that the notion of "moral duty" seems a bit archaic in this age of indulgence, but it is a concept that is at the heart of the Christian faith. If our age is an age of the anti-hero and the loss of heroism, perhaps it has something to do with the eclipse of the virtue of duty. It is at this point that the Christian pastor faces a doubly unpleasant task. He has a duty to perform: to inform the couple he is counseling of their duty. He has a duty to teach about duty. This is what obedience is all about.

Dealing with Contemporary Divorce Mythology

One of the tasks of the Christian is to distinguish between reality and myth. If we are going to manifest the wisdom of Christ in this area, we must be about the business of demythologizing. When the secular world seeks justification for a distorted

divorce ethic it builds that justification on a plat-
form of myths.

*Myth 1—"When love has gone out of a marriage,
it is better to get divorced."* This myth is built
on several subjective assumptions. It assumes the
ability to judge that love has in fact left the marriage. It assumes that the love that has departed
has no hope of ever returning, that it is irretriev-
ably gone. How can anybody ever make such a
judgment about the future? What kind of love
are we talking about here? If we define the "departed love" in activistic-behavioral terms, why
must we think of it as being irrevocably gone?
Being loving in actions and behavior is an act
of the will and can be achieved by the sheer force
of duty if for no other reason. To be sure, it is
much easier to be loving if you're "in love," but
being "in love" is not intrinsically necessary to
being loving—else the Great Commandment is a
farce. Even if we define love in emotional terms
or feeling-states, we are still not able to predict
with accuracy what our feeling-states will be
toward someone in the future. When people change
in their attitudes and behavior toward us, we have
a tendency to change our feelings toward them.

One of the most common thoughts expressed
by people in the midst of divorce counseling is
the idea that "not only do I not love my spouse,
but actually I've never been in love with her/him.
This was a mistake from the beginning." This kind
of thinking involves a projection of feelings back-
ward to the past. When people tell me this, I ask
them if their parents forced them to get married.
The answer is usually "no." I ask them if they

were ever attracted to their spouse during dating, etc. Usually with very little probing the person is able to see that in fact there was a time that they were very much in love with their spouse and that they were getting their present feelings all mixed up and confused with their memories of the distant past. These people are projecting their present feelings both to the past and future, being convinced that these feelings can never change again.

Myth 2—"It is better for the children if the unhappy couple divorce than to raise their children in the atmosphere of an unhappy marriage." This myth is so persistent and has been repeated so many times that people often accept it uncritically as a truism. There are a host of problems connected with this myth. Let us consider a few of them. In the first place, how can we possibly measure the impact of divorce or continuation of marriage on child development in particular cases? We can, of course, study the problems of child development in broken homes and in unhappy homes and compare the results generally. Such studies of broken homes have been grim to say the least and give little credibility that the divorce is a positive factor in child development. But such studies can give us only a wide generalization as a basis for projection in a given circumstance. When we study a child's development after divorce breaks the home, how can we know what that development would have been had the parents not divorced? This involves an examination of *conditions contrary to fact* which add little to scientific knowledge. By the nature of the case such an examination would involve an enormous amount of subjective speculation.

Secondly, it might be helpful to ask the children what they think about the truth of the myth. I have yet to hear a child express the desire for his parents to divorce in order that his own home life might be improved. Perhaps there are children who feel that way, but I am inclined to think they represent a very small minority.

Thirdly, why is it better for the children if the couple divorce? Obviously divorce would mean a reduction in the level of child exposure to parental arguments which can be traumatic, etc. But how do we measure the benefits of such a reduction against the loss of the presence in the home of a father or mother?

Fourthly, the judgment that it is better for the children if the parents divorce is usually couched in terms of a false dilemma. That is, it assumes that there are again only two alternatives: broken home or a home that has an unhealthy atmosphere of arguments, etc. The fallacy of this false dilemma will be explored more fully when we consider the myth of divorce being the "lesser of two evils."

Finally, it is important to realize that in hard cold reality it is the rare person who seeks divorce on the basis of a concern for the well-being of the children. What is distressing about this myth is not so much the fallacy of it as its blatant expression of hypocrisy. If people were really concerned for the well-being of their children, I would think they would move heaven and earth to transcend their false dilemma and move in the direction of responsible parenthood. With the use of this myth as a justification for divorce, mankind exposes his own capacity for calling good evil and evil good. Here an act of selfishness is painted or portrayed as a noble act of self-sacrifice for the good of the children.

Myth 3—"Divorce is the lesser of two evils." Closely related to Myth 2, this myth is built upon the false dilemma. Hear the words of Bruce Larson of Faith at Work as he articulates the myth:

> It may be that divorce is a way out for both. To stay married for the sake of the children does irreparable harm to the children and there is no justification for that. To stay married in order to fulfill some law of God that destroys people is no law of God. And even though it is not what God planned for man, it may be better than staying married to someone you wish were dead, for that is murder, or imagining that you are married to someone else, for that is adultery.[1]

Indeed it was a shock and profound disappointment to read these lines from Bruce Larson. That secular mythology has permeated the thinking of this man only underlines how subtle it can be. Larson admits that the Scripture is clear on the matter of divorce, but he adds that when a couple can no longer live together creatively they are forced to choose the lesser of two evils, i.e., divorce. Larson with one breath affirms the correctness of the teaching of Christ and in the next adds a new ground for divorce—the loss of the ability for creativity. Again the false dilemma principle is in effect. Larson assumes only two alternatives: the intolerable status quo or divorce. His logic is weak. Condider his argument.

Premise A—Staying married does irreparable damage to children.

---

1. Bruce Larson, *Ask Me to Dance*, p. 98.

Premise B—There's no justification for doing irreparable damage to children.
Conclusion—Divorce is a way out.

His argument is based on the combined fallacies
of Myth 2 and Myth 3. If we follow his logic we
must conclude that divorce is not only permissible
in certain situations but morally necessary. This
is situation ethics in its most crass form.

The fallacy of the false dilemma may be seen
in a simple illustration. Suppose I sign a commer-
cial contract (or covenant) whereby I promise to
pay the other party $10,000 for a piece of equipment
or a job to be done. The party produces the equipment or does the job and then sends me the bill
for $10,000. Now I have $10,000 in the bank, but
if I give him the $10,000, I will have to make costly
sacrifices in my life-style, etc. I want to keep on
living as I am, but I can't do that and pay the
$10,000. I may be able to maintain my life-style
if I pay the man $5,000 and renege on the rest.
So I send him a check for $5,000 and explain to
him that it would be too painful for me to abide
by my original commitment, but at least I can
give half what I owe. It is certainly better than
paying nothing. Paying half what you owe is certainly a lesser evil than paying nothing—but it
can hardly be justified if the possibility exists of
paying it all.

Myth 4—"You owe it to yourself." From
Aynn Rand's philosophy of "egoism" to the popular notion of doing your own thing," we have seen
a revival of "enlightened self-interest" ethics in
our culture. We begin with the American truism
that every individual has an inalienable *right* to
the pursuit of happiness. We move quickly to the

conclusion that we have an inalienable right not only to the pursuit but to the achievement or possession of happiness. If that happiness is not easily attained, we move to a posture of demand. Not only *may* we be happy but we *must* be happy. It is not difficult to move to the next step: I am morally responsible to *be* happy. Not only is happiness a right, but now it is a duty! If I am not utterly happy in my marriage, then "I owe it to myself" to be happy. To *owe* something is to be under obligation to pay the debt.

The mythological character of this "truism" may be seen by simply examining the gratuitous leaps of judgment that are revealed in the thinking process. Beyond the obvious, however, is the important factor that the individual involved in a marriage covenant is not living in isolation with responsibilities only to himself. The fact remains that the individual has made a promise, a pledge, a vow to another person. Until that vow is fulfilled and the promise is kept, the individual is in debt to his marriage partner. There is where the debt is located. "You owe it to yourself" is not an excuse for breaking a marriage vow. This "truism" is merely a euphemism for a creed of selfishness. It betrays the human ingenuity for the fabrication of excuses. It is the fruit of rationalization, not honest evaluation.

Myth 5—"Everyone's entitled to one mistake." There is a popular folk saying that goes, "If you repeat a lie often enough, people will begin to believe it." This is the flip side of "You can fool all the people part of the time, and some of the people all of the time, but you can't fool all of the people all of the time." The ease with which people can be fooled by repeating the lie is the bedrock of Madison Avenue and the advertising industry. It is popularly employed by the crass politician and the proverbial used-car dealer. But the marriage state is not a used-car lot. This kind of thinking won't do for dealing with the serious business of the home.

Let's examine the slogan. Is everyone entitled to one mistake? Are we all entitled to one murder? one kidnapping? one rape? etc.? Am I entitled to one act of infidelity to my wife? Is it my right to break up one home and leave one child without a father? May I stand before God and say, "I am entitled to break one vow I made before you"?

Who or what is it that entitles us to one mistake? Where did we ever get such a notion? Why only one mistake? Why not "everyone is entitled to ten mistakes"? Even if we granted this absurd premise, it wouldn't help in the divorce question. When people file for divorce it is not usually an expression of their first mistake. I am confident that most people have used up their "one mistake" by the time they're married, not to mention by the time they go to divorce court.

Again the term "mistake" is a euphemism. It is easier to say "I made a mistake" than to say "I sinned." The word "mistake" softens the seriousness of the crime. When Richard M. Nixon announced to the American people his resignation as President of the United States, he said, "I made a mistake." But the nation was not satisfied with that kind of "confession" and that kind of "repentance."

God is certainly slow to anger and quick to forgive our sins. He is more than willing to give us a second chance and more. Though forgiveness

154

is offered us freely, it would be a gross distortion of that kindness to assume therefore that we are entitled to sin.

Myth 6—"God led me to this divorce." If I hadn't heard this with my own ears on numerous occasions from professing Christians, I would be hard pressed to believe that any Christian would ever have the audacity to claim that God the Holy Spirit has led him into disobedience. But I've heard it too many times to be surprised by it anymore. The most astonishing thing about this myth is that some Christians actually believe it.

This is a classical example of the double standard: God reveals His law for His people in His Word, but He cancels His moral law for special exempt persons by means of "private revelations." This myth leaves us with a God who speaks with a forked tongue.

Obviously this myth is not initiated by heaven but finds its impetus in the subjective desires of the confused soul of man. The myth is based not upon truth but on wish-projection. I move from wishing that God would allow me to do something to allowing myself to do it, to claiming divine approval for it until I finally convince myself that God not only allows and approves my action but actually recommended it in the first place.

The myth is very effective in manipulating other Christians. Many Christians are very reluctant to challenge the claims of their friends' personal spiritual "leadings." By declaring that the Spirit has led me to a particular action, I can disobey God and appear very "spiritual" at the same time. It is one thing to shift the blame for my sin to another human being, but to shift it to God borders upon (and often transgresses the border of) blasphemy.

To illustrate how confused we can become with our own feelings, wishes, prayers, I will relate the following incident.

A woman asked to apeak with me concerning a problem in her marriage. She was greatly distessed as she related her story. She had been married to her husband for forty years. For that entire period she was a Christian and her husband was not. In between fits of weeping the woman told me of all the difficulties the mixed marriage had produced. She said her husband was a good provider, was faithful, etc., but they didn't share the same ultimate values. Consequently they were brought into frequent conflict. She expressed that she had carried the burden of the mixed marriage long enough. She had endured forty years, had seen the children through college and married, and had had enough. Consequently, she went on, she had moved out and left her husband two weeks previous to our meeting.

The immediate crisis she was facing was that her husband was phoning her every day and begging her with tearful pleas to return home. She said, "Every day for the past two weeks I have been praying desperately that God would show me His will. Please, Mr. Sproul, tell me what the will of God is. What can I do?"

I replied as gently as I could, "The first thing you can do is to stop praying about the will of God in this matter. God has already declared His will in this matter by forbidding us from departing from our unbelieving spouses."

The change in the woman's mood was abrupt

and instantaneous. From a spirit of brokenness and desperation she changed to a posture of unbridled fury. In a word, she was enraged. She hurled at me, "How can you say that? You don't live with that man. You wouldn't be able to put up with a marriage partner like mine. How easy it is for you to stand there and tell me what the will of God is!" As I said, she was very angry with me.

I admitted the truth or at least the probable truth of what she was saying. I told her that it was possible that I would have bailed out of such an unpleasant situation even before she did. However, I reminded her that the question she asked me was not what I would do it I were in her situation. The question she asked was what the will of God was in the matter. When I had responded she said that was easy for me to say what the will of God was. That charge was half right. It was easy for me to *know* what the will of God was since God's Word was crystal clear on the matter. It was not, however, easy for me to *say* what I said because I knew very well it was not what she wanted me to say.

The woman finally calmed down. With a new sense of duty and determination she returned to her husband. Fortunately this woman stopped short of the fantasy that God had told her to leave him. She realized finally that her prayer for the will of God had been not so much a prayer that God would reveal His will to her but that God would rescind His will and grant her a special exemption from her Christian duty.

It becomes necessary at times for every Christian to do things that are contrary to one's desires.

Perhaps no human situation is more difficult to deal with in terms of the conflict of God's will and our own interests than the situation of marriage or divorce.

Marriage is established and regulated by a God of truth. The problems of marriage cannot be resolved by myths. It is the truth that liberates and the truth that redeems. That is as true for marriage as it is for all of life.

Questions for Discussion

1. How do you account for the increase of the divorce rate in America?

2. What was the issue in the debate over divorce between Jesus and the Pharisees?

3. Is there such a thing as "spiritual adultery"? Is it a legitimate ground for divorce?

4. If a professing Christian deserts his spouse and does not repent, should the church declare the deserter an "unbeliever"?

5. What can be done to change the direction of a marriage?

6. Can "love" ever be restored to a marriage once it has gone?

7. Is divorce always the "lesser of two evils"?

8. When our desires conflict with our vows, what should we do?

9. Does the Holy Spirit lead to disobedience?